S0-ACV-484

Laughter and Misadventure
in the Middle East . . .

Books by Agatha Christie

Published by POCKET BOOKS

Agatha Christie Mallowan

Come, Tell Me How You Live

PUBLISHED BY POCKET BOOKS NEW YORK

POCKET BOOKS, a Simon & Schuster division of
GULF & WESTERN CORPORATION
1230 Avenue of the Americas, New York, N.Y. 10020

ISBN: 0-671-43282-6

First Pocket Books printing October, 1977

10 9 8 7 6 5 4

POCKET and colophon are trademarks of Simon & Schuster.

Printed in the U.S.A.

To my husband, Max Mallowan; to the Colonel, Bumps, Mac and Guilford, this meandering chronicle is affectionately dedicated.

SYRIA
and
MESOPOTAMIA

CONTENTS

A-SITTING ON A TELL

(With apologies to Lewis Carroll)

I'll tell you everything I can
   If you will listen well:
I met an erudite young man
   A-sitting on a Tell.
"Who are you, sir?" to him I said,
   "For what is it you look?"
His answer trickled through my head
   Like bloodstains in a book.

He said: "I look for aged pots
   Of prehistoric days,
And then I measure them in lots
   And lots of different ways.
And then (like you) I start to write,
   My words are twice as long
As yours, and far more erudite.
   They prove my colleagues wrong!"

But I was thinking of a plan
   To kill a millionaire

And hide the body in a van
    Or some large Frigidaire.
So, having no reply to give,
    And feeling rather shy,
I cried: "Come, tell me how you live!
    And when, and where, and why?"

His accents mild were full of wit:
    "Five thousand years ago
Is really, when I think of it,
    The choicest Age I know.
And once you learn to scorn A.D.
    And you have got the knack,
Then you could come and dig with me
    And never wander back."

But I was thinking how to thrust
    Some arsenic into tea,
And could not all at once adjust
    My mind so far B.C.
I looked at him and softly sighed,
    His face was pleasant too. . . .
"Come, tell me how you live?" I cried,
    "And what it is you do?"

He said: "I hunt for objects made
    By men where'er they roam,
I photograph and catalog
    And pack and send them home.
These things we do not sell for gold
    (Nor yet, indeed, for copper!),
But place them on Museum shelves
    As only right and proper.

"I sometimes dig up amulets
    And figurines most lewd,
For in those prehistoric days
    They were extremely rude!
And that's the way we take our fun,
    'Tis not the way of wealth.

But archaeologists live long
  And have the rudest health."

I heard him then, for I had just
  Completed a design
To keep a body free from dust
  By boiling it in brine.
I thanked him much for telling me
  With so much erudition,
And said that I would go with him
  Upon an Expedition. . . .

And now, if e'er by chance I dip
  My fingers into acid,
Or smash some pottery (with slip!)
  Because I am not placid,
Or if I see a river flow
  And hear a far-off yell,
I sigh, for it reminds me so
  Of that young man I learned to know——

Whose look was mild, whose speech was slow,
Whose thoughts were in the long ago,
Whose pockets sagged with potsherds so,
Who lectured learnedly and low,
Who used long words I didn't know,
Whose eyes, with fervor all a-glow,
Upon the ground looked to and fro,
Who sought conclusively to show
That there were things I ought to know
And that with him I ought to go
  And dig upon a Tell!

FOREWORD

THIS BOOK IS an answer. It is the answer to a question that is asked me very often.

"So you dig in Syria, do you? Do tell me all about it. How do you live? In a tent?" etc., etc.

Most people, probably, do not want to know. It is just the small change of conversation. But there are, now and then, one or two people who are really interested.

It is the question, too, that Archaeology asks of the Past—*Come, tell me how you lived?*

And with picks and spades and baskets we find the answer.

"These were our cooking pots." "In this big silo we kept our grain." "With these bone needles we sewed our clothes." "These were our houses, this our bath-room, here our system of sanitation!" "Here, in this pot, are the gold ear-rings of my daughter's dowry." "Here, in this little jar, is my make-up." "All these cook-pots are of a very common type. You'll find them by the hundred. We get them from the Potter at the

corner. Woolworth's, did you say? Is that what you call him in your time?"

Occasionally there is a Royal Palace, sometimes a Temple, much more rarely a Royal burial. These things are spectacular. They appear in newspapers in headlines, are lectured about, shown on screens, everybody hears of them! Yet I think to one engaged in digging, the real interest is in the everyday life—the life of the potter, the farmer, the tool-maker, the expert cutter of animal seals and amulets—in fact, *the butcher, the baker, the candlestick-maker.*

A final warning, so that there will be no disappointment. This is not a profound book—it will give you no interesting sidelights on archaeology, there will be no beautiful descriptions of scenery, no treating of economic problems, no racial reflections, no history.

It is, in fact, small beer—a very little book, full of everyday doings and happenings.

Come, Tell Me
How You Live

I

PARTANT POUR LA SYRIE

IN A FEW weeks' time we are starting for Syria!

Shopping for a hot climate in autumn or winter presents certain difficulties. One's last year's summer clothes, which one has optimistically hoped will "do," do not "do" now the time has come. For one thing they appear to be (like the depressing annotations in furniture removers' lists) "Bruised, Scratched and Marked." (And also Shrunk, Faded and Peculiar!) For another —alas, alas that one has to say it!—they are too tight everywhere.

So—to the shops and the stores, and:

"Of course, Modom, we are not being asked for that kind of thing just *now!* We have some very charming little suits here—O.S. in the darker colors."

Oh, loathsome O.S.! How humiliating to be O.S.! How even more humiliating to be recognized at once as O.S.!

(Although there are better days when, wrapped in a lean long black coat with a large fur collar, a saleswoman says cheeringly:

17

"But *surely* Modom is *only* a Full Woman?")

I look at the little suits, with their dabs of unexpected fur and their pleated skirts. I explain sadly that what I want is a washing silk or cotton.

"Modom might try Our Cruising Department."

Modom tries Our Cruising Department—but without any exaggerated hopes. Cruising is still enveloped in the realms of romantic fancy. It has a touch of Arcady about it. It is girls who go cruising—girls who are slim and young and wear uncrushable linen trousers, immensely wide round the feet and skintight round the hips. It is girls who sport delightfully in Play Suits. It is girls for whom Shorts of eighteen different varieties are kept!

The lovely creature in charge of Our Cruising Department is barely sympathetic.

"Oh, no, Modom, we do not keep *out*-sizes." (Faint horror! Outsizes and Cruising? Where is the romance there?)

She adds:

"It would hardly be *suitable,* would it?"

I agree sadly that it would not be suitable.

There is still one hope. There is Our Tropical Department.

Our Tropical Department consists principally of Topees—Brown Topees, White Topees; Special Patent Topees. A little to one side, as being slightly frivolous, are Double Terais, blossoming in pinks and blues and yellows like blooms of strange tropical flowers. There is also an immense wooden horse and an assortment of jodhpurs.

But—yes—there are other things. Here is suitable wear for the wives of Empire Builders. Shantung! Plainly cut shantung coats and skirts—no girlish nonsense here—bulk is accommodated as well as scragginess! I depart into a cubicle with various styles and sizes. A few minutes later I am transformed into a Memsahib!

I have certain qualms—but stifle them. After all, it *is* cool and practical and I *can* get into it.

I turn my attention to the selection of the right kind of hat. The right kind of hat not existing in these days, I have to have it made for me. This is not so easy as it sounds.

What I want, and what I mean to have, and what I shall almost certainly not get, is a felt hat of reasonable proportions that will fit on my head. It is the kind of hat that was worn some twenty years ago for taking the dogs for a walk or playing a round of golf. Now, alas, there are only the Things one attaches to one's head—over one eye, one ear, on the nape of one's neck—as the fashion of the moment dictates— or the Double Terai, measuring at least a yard across.

I explain that I want a hat with a crown like a Double Terai and about a quarter of its brim.

"But they are made wide to protect fully from the sun, Modom."

"Yes, but where I am going there is nearly always a terrific wind, and a hat with a brim won't stay on one's head for a minute."

"We could put Modom on an elastic."

"I want a hat with a brim no larger than this that I've got on."

"Of course, Modom, with a shallow crown that would look quite well."

"*Not* a shallow crown! The hat has got To Keep On!"

Victory! We select the color—one of those new shades with the pretty names: Dirt, Rust, Mud, Pavement, Dust, etc.

A few minor purchases—purchases that I know instinctively will either be useless or land me in trouble. A Zip travelling bag, for instance. Life, nowadays is dominated and complicated by the remorseless Zip. Blouses zip up, skirts zip down, ski-ing suits zip everywhere. "Little frocks" have perfectly unnecessary bits of zipping on them just for fun.

Why? Is there anything more deadly than a Zip that turns nasty on you? It involves you in a far worse predicament than any ordinary button, clip, snap, buckle or hook and eye.

In the early days of Zips, my mother, thrilled by this delicious novelty, had a pair of corsets fashioned for her which zipped up the front. The results were unfortunate in the extreme! Not only was the original zipping-up fraught with extreme agony, but the corsets then obstinately refused to de-zip! Their removal was practically a surgical operation! And owing to my mother's delightful Victorian modesty, it seemed possible for a while that she would live in these corsets for the remainder of her life—a kind of modern Woman in the Iron Corset!

I have therefore always regarded the Zip with a wary eye. But it appears that *all* travelling bags have Zips.

"The old-fashioned fastening is quite superseded, Modom," says the salesman, regarding me with a pitying look.

"This, you see, is so simple," he says, demonstrating.

There is no doubt about its simplicity—but then, I think to myself, the bag is empty.

"Well," I say, sighing, "one must move with the times."

With some misgivings I buy the bag.

I am now the proud possessor of a Zip travelling bag, an Empire Builder's Wife's coat and skirt, and a possibly satisfactory hat.

There is still much to be done.

I pass to the Stationery Department. I buy several fountain and stylographic pens—it being my experience that, though a fountain pen in England behaves in an exemplary manner, the moment it is let loose in desert surroundings it perceives that it is at liberty to go on strike and behaves accordingly, either spouting ink indiscriminately over me, my clothes, my notebook and anything else handy, or else coyly refusing to do anything but scratch invisibly across the surface of the paper. I also buy a modest two pencils. Pencils are, fortunately, not temperamental, and though given to a

knack of quiet disappearance, I have always a resource
at hand. After all, what is the use of an architect if
not to borrow pencils from?

Four wrist-watches is the next purchase. The desert
is not kind to watches. After a few weeks there, one's
watch gives up steady everyday work. Time, it says, is
only a mode of thought. It then takes its choice between stopping eight or nine times a day for periods of
twenty minutes, or of racing indiscriminately ahead.
Sometimes it alternates coyly between the two. It
finally stops altogether. One then goes on to wrist-
watch No. 2, and so on. There is also a purchase of
two four and six watches in readiness for that moment
when my husband will say to me: "Just lend me a
watch to give to the foreman, will you?"

Our Arab foremen, excellent though they are, have
what might be described as a heavy hand with any
kind of timepiece. Telling the time, anyway, calls for
a good deal of mental strain on their part. They can
be seen holding a large round moon-faced watch earnestly upside down, and gazing at it with really painful
concentration while they get the answer wrong! Their
winding of these treasures is energetic and so thorough
that few mainsprings can stand up to the strain!

It therefore happens that by the end of the season
the watches of the expedition staff have been sacrificed
one by one. My two four and six watches are a means
of putting off the evil day.

Packing!

There are several schools of thought as to packing.
There are the people who begin packing at anything
from a week or a fortnight beforehand. There are the
people who throw a few things together half an hour
before departure. There are the careful packers, in-
satiable for tissue paper! There are those who scorn
tissue paper and just throw the things in and hope for
the best! There are the packers who leave practically
everything that they want behind! And there are the

packers who take immense quantities of things that
they never will need!

One thing can safely be said about an archaeological
packing. It consists mainly of *books*. What books to
take, what books *can* be taken, what books are there
room for, what books can (with agony!) be left behind.
I am firmly convinced that all archaeologists pack in
the following manner: They decide on the maximum
number of suitcases that a long-suffering Wagon Lit
Company will permit them to take. They then fill these
suitcases to the brim with books. They then, reluctantly,
take out a few books, and fill in the space thus obtained with shirts, pajamas, socks, etc.

Looking into Max's room, I am under the impression that the whole cubic space is filled with books!
Through a chink in the books I catch sight of Max's
worried face.

"Do you think," he asks, "that I shall have room
for all these?"

The answer is so obviously in the negative that it
seems sheer cruelty to say it.

At 4:30 P.M. he arrives in my room and asks hopefully: "Any room in your suitcases?"

Long experience should have warned me to answer
firmly "No," but I hesitate, and immediately doom falls
upon me.

"If you could just get in one or two things——"

"Not *books?*"

Max looks faintly surprised and says: "Of course
books—what else?"

Advancing, he rams down two immense tomes on
top of the Empire Builder's Wife's suit which has been
lying smugly on top of a suitcase.

I utter a cry of protest, but too late.

"Nonsense," says Max, "lots of room!" And forces
down the lid, which refuses spiritedly to shut.

"It's not really full even now," says Max optimistically.

He is, fortunately, diverted at this moment by a

printed linen frock lying folded in another suitcase. "What's that?"

I reply that it is a dress.

"Interesting," says Max. "It's got fertility *motifs* all down the front."

One of the more uncomfortable things about being married to an archaeologist is their expert knowledge of the derivation of the most harmless looking patterns!

At five-thirty Max casually remarks that he'd better go out and buy a few shirts and socks and things. He returns three-quarters of an hour later, indignant because the shops all shut at six. When I say they always do, he replies that he had never noticed it before.

Now, he says, he has nothing to do but "clear up his papers."

At 11 P.M. I retire to bed, leaving Max at his desk (never to be tidied or dusted under the most dire penalties), up to the elbows in letters, bills, pamphlets, drawings of pots, innumerable potsherds, and various match-boxes, none of them containing matches, but instead odd beads of great antiquity.

At 4 A.M. he comes excitedly into the bedroom, cup of tea in hand, to announce that he has at last found that very interesting article on Anatolian finds which he had lost last July. He adds that he hopes that he hasn't woken me up.

I say that of course he has woken me up, and he'd better get me a cup of tea too!

Returning with the tea, Max says he has also found a great many bills which he thought he had paid. I, too, have had that experience. We agree that it is depressing.

At 9 A.M. I am called in as the heavy-weight to sit on Max's bulging suitcases.

"If *you* can't make them shut," says Max ungallantly, "nobody can!"

The superhuman feat is finally accomplished by the aid of sheer avoirdupois, and I return to contend with my own difficulty, which is, as prophetic vision had told me it would be, the Zip bag. Empty in Mr. Gooch's shop, it had looked simple, attractive, and labor-saving. How merrily then had the Zip run to and fro! Now, full to the brim, the closing of it is a miracle of super-human adjustment. The two edges have to be brought together with mathematical precision, and then, just as the Zip is traveling slowly across, complications set in, due to the corner of a sponge-bag. When at last it closes, I vow not to open it again until I get to Syria!

On reflection, however, this is hardly possible. What about the aforementioned sponge-bag. Am I to travel for five days unwashed? At the moment even *that* seems preferable to unzipping the Zip bag!

Yes, now the moment has come and we are really off. Quantities of important things have been left un-done: the Laundry, as usual, has let us down; the Cleaners, to Max's chagrin, have not kept their prom-ises—but what does anything matter? We are going!

Just for a moment or two it looks as though we weren't going! Max's suitcases, delusive in appearance, are beyond the powers of the taximan to lift. He and Max struggle with them, and finally, with the assistance of a passer-by, they are hoisted on to the taxi.

We drive off for Victoria.

Dear Victoria—gateway to the world beyond En-gland—how I love your continental platform. And how I love trains, anyway! Snuffing up the sulphurous smell ecstatically—so different from the faint, aloof, distantly oily smell of a boat, which always depresses my spirits with its prophecy of nauseous days to come. But a train—a big snorting, hurrying, companionable train, with its big puffing engine, sending up clouds of steam, and seeming to say impatiently: "I've got to be off, I've got to be off, I've *got* to be off!"—is a friend! It shares your mood, for you, too, are saying: "I'm going to be off, I'm going, I'm going, I'm *going . . .*"

By the door of our Pullman, friends are waiting to see us off. The usual idiotic conversations take place. Famous last words pour from my lips—instructions about dogs, about children, about forwarding letters, about sending out books, about forgotten items, "and I think you'll find it on the piano, but it *may* be on the bathroom shelf." All the things that have been said before, and do not in the least need saying again!

Max is surrounded by his relations, I by mine.

My sister says tearfully that she has a feeling that she will never see me again. I am not very much impressed, because she has felt this every time I go to the East. And what, she asks, is she to do if Rosalind gets appendicitis? There seems no reason why my fourteen-year-old daughter should get appendicitis, and all I can think of to reply is: "Don't operate on her yourself!" For my sister has a great reputation for hasty action with her scissors, attacking impartially boils, haircutting, and dressmaking—usually, I must admit, with great success.

Max and I exchange relations, and my dear mother-in-law urges me to take great care of myself, implying that I am nobly going into great personal danger.

Whistles blow, and I have a last few frenzied words with my friend and secretary. Will she do all the things I have left undone, and upbraid suitably the Laundry and the Cleaners and give a good reference to the cook and send off those books I couldn't pack, and get back my umbrella from Scotland Yard, and write appropriately to the clergyman who has discovered forty-three grammatical errors in my last book, and go through the seed-list for the garden and cross off vegetable marrows and parsnips? Yes, she will do all those things, and if any crisis occurs in the Home or the Literary World she will cable me. It doesn't matter, I say. She has a power of attorney. She can do anything she likes. She looks rather alarmed and says she shall be most careful. Another whistle! I say good-bye to my sister, and say wildly that I, too, feel I shall never see her again, and perhaps Rosalind *will* get appendicitis. Nonsense, says my sister; why should she? We climb into the Pullman, the train grunts and starts—we are OFF.

For about forty-five seconds I feel terrible, and then as Victoria Station is left behind, exultation springs up once more. We have begun the lovely, exciting journey to Syria.

There is something grand and stuck-up about a Pullman, though it is not nearly as comfortable as a corner of an ordinary first-class carriage. We always go by Pullman solely on account of Max's suitcases, which an ordinary carriage would not tolerate. Having once had registered luggage go astray, Max takes no chances with his precious books.

We arrive at Dover, to find the sea moderately calm. Nevertheless I retire to the Salon des Dames, and lie and meditate with the pessimism always induced in me by the motion of the waves. But we are soon at Calais, and the French steward produces a large blue-bloused man to deal with my luggage. "Madame will find him in the Douane," he says.

"What is his number?" I ask. The steward is immediately reproachful.

"Madame! Mais c'est le charpentier du bateau!"

I become properly abashed—to reflect a few minutes later that that is not really an answer. Why, because he is the *charpentier du bateau,* does it make it any easier to pick him out from several hundred other blue-bloused men, all shouting, *"Quatre-vingt treize?"* etc. His mere silence will not be sufficient identification. Moreover, does his being the *charpentier du bateau* enable him to pick out with unerring certainty one middle-aged Englishwoman from a whole crowd of middle-aged Englishwomen?

At this point in my reflections Max joins me, and says he has a porter for my luggage. I explain that the *charpentier du bateau* has taken mine, and Max asks why I let him. All the luggage should go together. I agree, but plead that my intellect is always weakened by sea-crossings. Max says: "Oh, well; we shall collect it all in the Douane." And we proceed to that inferno of yelling porters and to the inevitable encounter with the only type of really unpleasant Frenchwoman that exists—the Customs House Female; a being devoid of charm, of *chic,* of any feminine grace. She prods, she peers, she says, *"Pas de cigarettes?"* unbelievingly, and finally, with a reluctant grunt, she scrawls the mystic hieroglyphics in chalk on our baggage, and we pass through the barrier and out on to the platform, and so to the Simplon Orient Express and the journey across Europe.

Many, many years ago, when going to the Riviera or to Paris, I used to be fascinated by the sight of the Orient Express at Calais and longed to be travelling by it. Now it has become an old familiar friend, but the thrill has never quite died down. I am going by it! I am *in* it! I am actually in the blue coach, with the simple legend outside: CALAIS-ISTANBUL. It is, undoubtedly, my favorite train. I like its tempo, which, starting *Allegro con fuore,* swaying and rattling and hurling one from side to side in its mad haste to leave Calais and the Occident, gradually slows down in a *rallantando* as it proceeds eastwards till it becomes definitely *legato.*

In the early morning of the next day I let the blind up, and watch the dim shapes of the mountains in Switzerland, then the descent into the plains of Italy, passing by lovely Stresa and its blue lake. Then, later, into the smart station that is all we see of Venice and out again, and along by the sea to Trieste and so into Yugoslavia. The pace gets slower and slower, the stops are longer, the station clocks display conflicting times. H.E.O. is succeeded by C.E. The names of the stations are written in exciting and improbable looking letters. The engines are fat and comfortable looking, and belch forth a particularly black and evil smoke. Bills in the dining-cars are written out in perplexing currencies, and bottles of strange mineral water appear. A small Frenchman who sits opposite us at table studies his bill in silence for some minutes, then he raises his head and catches Max's eye. His voice, charged with emotion, rises plaintively: *"Le change des Wagons Lits, c'est incroyable!"* Across the aisle a dark man with a hooked nose demands to be told the amount of his bill in (*a*) francs, (*b*) lire, (*c*) dinars, (*d*) Turkish pounds, (*e*) dollars. When this has been done by the long-suffering restaurant attendant, the traveller calculates silently, and evidently a master financial brain, produces the currency most advantageous to his pocket. By this method, he explains to us, he has saved five-pence in English money!

In the morning Turkish Customs officials appear on the train. They are leisurely, and deeply interested in our baggage. Why, they ask me, have I so many pairs of shoes? It is too many. But, I reply, I have no cigarettes, because I do not smoke, so why not a few more shoes? The douanier accepts the explanation. It appears to him reasonable. What, he asks, is the powder in this little tin?

It is bug powder, I say; but find that this is not understood. He frowns and looks suspicious. He is obviously suspecting me of being a drug-smuggler. It is not powder for the teeth, he says accusingly, nor for the face; for *what,* then? Vivid pantomime by me! I scratch myself realistically, I catch the interloper. I sprinkle the woodwork. Ah, all is understood! He throws back his head and roars with laughter, repeating a Turkish word. It is for *them,* the powder! He repeats the joke to a colleague. They pass on, enjoying it very much. The Wagon Lit conductor now appears to coach us. They will come with our passports to demand how much money we have *"effectif, vous comprenez?"* I love the word *effectif*—it is so exactly descriptive of actual cash in hand. "You will have," the conductor proceeds, "exactly so much *effectif!*" He names the sum. Max objects that we have more than that. "It does not matter. To say so will cause you embarrassments. You will say you have the letter of credit or the travellers' cheques and of *effectif* so much." He adds in explanation: "They do not mind, you comprehend, *what* you have, but the answer must be *en règle.* You will say—so much."

Presently the gentleman in charge of the financial questions comes along. He writes down our answer before we actually say it. All is *en règle.* And now we are arriving at Stamboul, winding in and out through strange wooden slatted houses, with glimpses of heavy stone bastions and glimpses of sea at our right.

A maddening city, Stamboul—since when you are in it you can never see it! Only when you have left the European side and are crossing the Bosphorus to the Asian coast do you really see Stamboul. Very beautiful it is this morning—a clear, shining pale morning, with no mist, and the mosques with their minarets standing up against the sky.

"La Sainte Sophie, it is very fine," says a French gentleman.

Everybody agrees, with the regrettable exception of myself. I, alas, have never admired Sainte Sophie! An unfortunate lapse of taste; but there it is. It has always seemed definitely to me the wrong size. Ashamed of my perverted ideas, I keep silent.

Now into the waiting train at Haidar Pacha, and, when at last the train starts, breakfast—a breakfast for which one is by now quite ravenous! Then a lovely day's journey along the winding coast of the Sea of Marmora, with islands dotted about looking dim and lovely. I think for the hundredth time that I should like to own one of those islands. Strange the desire for an island of one's own! Most people suffer from it sooner or later. It symbolises in one's mind liberty, solitude, freedom from all cares. Yet actually, I suppose, it would mean not liberty but imprisonment. One's housekeeping would probably depend entirely on the mainland. One would be continually writing long lists of grocery orders for the stores, arranging for meat and bread, doing all one's housework, since few domestics would care to live on an island far from friends or cinemas, without even a bus communication with their fellow-kind. A South Sea island, I always

imagined, would be different! There one would sit, idly
eating the best kinds of fruit, dispensing with plates,
knives, forks, washing up, and the problem of grease
on the sink! Actually the only South Sea islanders I
ever saw having a meal were eating platefuls of hot
beef stew rolling in grease, all set on a very dirty tablecloth.

No; an island is, and should be, a dream island! On
that island there is no sweeping, dusting, bedmaking,
laundry, washing up, grease, food problems, lists of
groceries, lamp-trimming, potato-peeling, dustbins. On
the dream island there is white sand and blue sea—
and a fairy house, perhaps, built between sunrise and
sunset; the apple tree, the singing and the gold. . . .

At this point in my reflections, Max asks me what
I am thinking about. I say, simply, "Paradise!"

Max says: "Ah, wait till you see the Jaghjagha!"

I ask if it is very beautiful; and Max says he has no
idea, but it is a remarkably interesting part of the
world and nobody really knows anything about it!

The train winds its way up a gorge, and we leave
the sea behind us.

The next morning we reach the Cilician Gates, and
look out over one of the most beautiful views I know.
It is like standing on the rim of the world and looking
down on the promised land, and one feels much as
Moses must have felt. For here, too, there is no en-
tering in. . . . The soft, hazy dark blue loveliness is a
land one will never reach; the actual towns and villages
when one gets there will be only the ordinary everyday
world—not this enchanted beauty that beckons you
down. . . .

The train whistles. We climb back into our compartment.

On to Alep. And from Alep to Beyrout, where our
architect is to meet us and where things are to get
under way, for our preliminary survey of the Habur
and Jaghjagha region, which will lead to the selection
of a mound suitable for excavation.

For this, like Mrs. Beeton, is the start of the whole

business. First catch your hare, says that estimable lady.

So, in our case, first find your mound. That is what we are about to do.

II

A SURVEYING TRIP

BEYROUT! BLUE SEA, a curving bay, a long coastline of hazy blue mountains. Such is the view from the terrace of the Hotel. From my bedroom, which looks inland, I see a garden of scarlet poinsettias. The room is high, distempered white, slightly prison-like in aspect. A modern wash-basin complete with taps and waste-pipe strikes a dashing modern note.[1] Above the basin and connected to the taps is a large square tank with removable lid. Inside, it is full of stale-smelling water, connected to the cold tap only!

The arrival of plumbing in the East is full of pitfalls. How often does the cold tap produce hot water, and the hot tap cold! And how well do I remember a bath in a newly equipped "Western" bathroom where an intimidating hot-water system produced scalding water in terrific quantities, no cold water was obtainable, the hot-water tap would not turn off, and the bolt of the door had stuck!

[1] This was written a time before the opening of the modern Hôtel St. George.

As I contemplate the poinsettias enthusiastically and the washing facilities distastefully, there is a knock at the door. A short, squat Armenian appears, smiling ingratiatingly. He opens his mouth, points a finger down his throat, and utters encouragingly *"Manger!"*

By this simple expedient he makes it clear to the meanest intelligence that luncheon is served in the dining-room.

There I find Max awaiting me, and our new architect, Mac, whom as yet I hardly know. In a few days' time we are to set off on a three months' camping expedition to examine the country for likely sites. With us, as guide, philosopher, and friend, is to go Hamoudi, for many years foreman at Ur, an old friend of my husband's, and who is to come with us between seasons in these autumn months.

Mac rises and greets me politely, and we sit down to a very good if slightly greasy meal. I make a few would-be amiable remarks to Mac, who blocks them effectively by replying: "Oh, yes?" "Really?" "Indeed?"

I find myself somewhat damped. An uneasy conviction sweeps over me that our young architect is going to prove one of those people who from time to time succeed in rendering me completely imbecile with shyness. I have, thank goodness, long left behind me the days when I was shy of *everyone*. I have attained, with middle age, a fair amount of poise and *savoir faire*. Every now and then I congratulate myself that all that silly business is over and done with! "I've got over it," I say to myself happily. And as surely as I think so, some unexpected individual reduces me once more to nervous idiocy.

Useless to tell myself that young Mac is probably extremely shy himself and that it is his own shyness which produces his defensive armor, the fact remains that, before his coldly superior manner, his gently raised eyebrows, his air of polite attention to words that I realize cannot possibly be worth listening to, I wilt visibly, and find myself talking what I fully realize is sheer nonsense. Towards the end of the meal Mac administers a reproof.

"Surely," he says gently in reply to a desperate statement of mine about the French Horn, "that is not so?"

He is, of course, perfectly right. It is not so.

After lunch, Max asks me what I think of Mac. I reply guardedly that he doesn't seem to talk much. That, says Max, is an excellent thing. I have no idea, he says, what it is like to be stuck in the desert with someone who never stops talking! "I chose him because he seemed a silent sort of fellow."

I admit there is something in that. Max goes on to say that he is probably shy, but will soon open up. "He's probably terrified of *you*," he adds kindly.

I consider this heartening thought, but don't feel convinced by it.

I try, however, to give myself a little mental treatment.

First of all, I say to myself, you are old enough to be Mac's mother. You are also an authoress—a well-known authoress. Why, one of your characters has even been the clue in a *Times* crossword. (High-water mark of fame!) And what is more, you are the wife of the Leader of the Expedition! Come now, if any one is to snub any one, it is *you* who will snub the young man, not the young man who will snub you.

Later, we decide to go out to tea, and I go along to Mac's room to ask him to come with us. I determine to be natural and friendly.

The room is unbelievably neat, and Mac is sitting on a folded plaid rug writing in his diary. He looks up in polite inquiry.

"Won't you come out with us and have tea?"

Mac rises.

"Thank you!"

"Afterwards, I expect you'd like to explore the town," I suggest. "It's fun poking round a new place."

Mac raises his eyebrows gently and says coldly: "Is it?"

Somewhat deflated, I lead the way to the hall where Max is waiting for us. Mac consumes a large tea in happy silence. Max is eating tea in the present, but his mind is roughly about 4000 B.C.

He comes out of his reverie with a sudden start as the last cake is eaten, and suggests that we go and see how our lorry is getting on.

We go forthwith to look at our lorry—a Ford chassis, to which a native body is being built. We have had to fall back on this as no second-hand one was to be obtained in sufficiently good condition.

The bodywork seems definitely optimistic, of the "Inshallah" nature, and the whole thing has a high and dignified appearance that is suspiciously too good to be true. Max is a little worried at the non-appearance of Hamoudi, who was to have met us in Beyrout by this date.

Mac scorns to look at the town and returns to his bedroom to sit on his rug and write in his diary. Interested speculation on my part as to what he writes in the diary.

An early awakening. At 5 A.M. our bedroom door opens, and a voice announces in Arabic: "Your foremen have come!"

Hamoudi and his two sons surge into the room with the eager charm that distinguishes them, seizing our hands, pressing them against their foreheads. "Shlon kefek?" (How is your comfort.) "Kullish zen." (Very well.) "El hamdu lillah! El hamdu lillah!" (We all praise God together!)

Shaking off the mists of sleep, we order tea, and Hamoudi and his sons squat down comfortably on the floor and proceed to exchange news with Max. The language barrier excludes me from this conversation. I have used all the Arabic I know. I long wistfully for sleep, and even wish that the Hamoudi family had postponed their greetings to a more reasonable hour. Still, I realize that to them it is the most natural thing in the world thus to arrive.

Tea dispels the mists of sleep, and Hamoudi addresses various remarks to me, which Max translates, as also my replies. All three of them beam with happiness, and I realize anew what very delightful people they are.

Preparations are now in full swing—buying of stores; engaging of a chauffeur and a cook; visits to the Service des Antiquités; a delightful lunch with M. Seyrig, the Director; and his very charming wife. Nobody could be kinder to us than they are—and, incidentally, the lunch is delicious.

Disagreeing with the Turkish Douanier's opinion that I have too many shoes, I proceed to buy more shoes! Shoes in Beyrout are a delight to buy. If your size is not available, they are made for you in a couple of days—of good leather, perfectly fitting. It must be admitted that buying shoes is a weakness of mine. I shall not dare to return home through Turkey!

We wander through the native quarters and buy interesting lengths of material—a kind of thick white silk, embroidered in golden thread or in dark blue. We buy silk *abas* to send home as presents. Max is fascinated with all the different kinds of bread. Any one with French blood in him loves good bread. Bread to a Frenchman means more than any other kind of food. I have heard an officer of the Services Spéciaux say of a colleague in a lonely frontier outpost: *"Ce pauvre garçon! Il n'a même pas de pain là bas, seulement la galette Kurde!"* with deep and heartfelt pity.

We also have long and complicated dealings with the Bank. I am struck, as always in the East, with the reluctance of banks to do any business whatever. They are polite, charming, but anxious to evade any actual transaction. *"Oui, oui!"* they murmur sympathetically. *"Ecrivez une lettre!"* And they settle down again with a sigh of relief at having postponed any action.

When action has been reluctantly forced upon them, they take revenge by a complicated system of *"les timbres."* Every document, every cheque, every transaction whatever, is held up and complicated by a demand for "les timbres." Continual small sums are disbursed. When everything is, as you think, finished, once more comes a hold-up!

"Et deux francs cinquante centimes pour les timbres, s'il vous plaît."

Still, at last transactions are completed, innumerable letters are written, incredible numbers of stamps are affixed. With a sigh of relief the Bank clerk sees a prospect of finally getting rid of us. As we leave the Bank, we hear him say firmly to another importunate client: *"Ecrivez une lettre, s'il vous plaît."*

There still remains the engaging of a cook and chauffeur.

The chauffeur problem is solved first. Hamoudi arrives, beaming, and informs us that we are in good fortune—he has secured for us an excellent chauffeur.

How, Max asks, has Hamoudi obtained this treasure?

Very simply, it appears. He was standing on the waterfront, and having had no job for some time, and being completely destitute, he will come very cheap. Thus, at once, we have effected an economy!

But is there any means of knowing whether he is a good chauffeur? Hamoudi waves such a question aside. A baker is a man who puts bread in an oven and bakes it. A chauffeur is a man who takes a car out and drives it!

Max, without any undue enthusiasm, agrees to engage Abdullah if nothing better offers, and Abdullah is summoned to an interview. He bears a remarkable resemblance to a camel, and Max says with a sigh that at any rate he seems stupid, and that is always satisfactory. I ask why, and Max says because he won't have the brains to be dishonest.

On our last afternoon in Beyrout we drive out to the Dog River, the Nahr el Kelb. Here, in a wooded gully running inland, is a café where you can drink coffee, and then wander pleasantly along a shady path.

But the real fascination of the Nahr el Kelb lies in the carved inscriptions on the rock where a pathway leads up to the pass over the Lebanon. For here, in countless wars, armies have marched and left their record. Here are Egyptian hieroglyphics—of Rameses II, and boasts made by Assyrian and Babylonian armies. There is the figure of Tiglathpileser I. Sennacherib left an inscription in 701 B.C. Alexander passed and left his record. Esarhaddon and Nebuchadrezzar have commemorated their victories and finally, linking up with antiquity, Allenby's army wrote names and initials in 1917. I never tire of looking at that carved surface of rock. Here is history made manifest. . . .

I am so far carried away as to remark enthusiastically to Mac that it is really very thrilling, and doesn't he think so?

Mac raises his polite eyebrows, and says in a completely uninterested voice that it is, of course, very interesting. . . .

The arrival and loading up of our lorry is the next excitement. The body of the lorry looks definitely top-heavy. It sways and dips, but has withal such an air of dignity—indeed of majesty—that it is promptly christened Queen Mary.

In addition to Queen Mary we hire a "taxi"—a Citröen driven by an amiable Armenian called Aristide. We engage a somewhat melancholy looking cook ('Isa), whose testimonials are so good as to be highly suspicious. And finally, the great day comes, and we set out—Max, Hamoudi, myself, Mac, Abdullah, Aristide and 'Isa—to be companions, for better, for worse, for the next three months.

Our first discovery is that Abdullah is quite the worst driver imaginable, our second is that the cook is a pretty bad cook, our third is that Aristide is a good driver but has an incredibly bad taxi!

We drive out of Beyrout along the coast road. We pass the Nahr el Kelb, and continue on with the sea on our left. We pass small clusters of white houses and entrancing little sandy bays, and small coves between rocks. I long to stop and bathe, but we have started now on the real business of life. Soon, too soon, we shall turn inland from the sea, and after that, for many months, we shall not see the sea again.

Aristide honks his horn ceaselessly in the Syrian fashion. Behind us Queen Mary is following, dipping and bending like a ship at sea with her top-heavy body-work.

We pass Byblos, and now the little clusters of white houses are few and far between. On our right is the rocky hillside.

And at last we turn off and strike inland for Homs.

There is a good hotel at Homs—a very fine hotel, Hamoudi has told us.

The grandeur of the hotel proves to be mainly in the building itself. It is spacious, with immense stone corridors. Its plumbing, alas, is not functioning very well! Its vast bedrooms contain little in the way of comfort. We look at ours respectfully, and then Max and I go out to see the town. Mac, we find, is sitting on the side of his bed, folded rug beside him, writing earnestly in his diary.

(*What* does Mac put in his diary? He displays no enthusiasm to have a look at Homs.)

Perhaps he is right, for there is not very much to see.

We have a badly cooked pseudo-European meal and retire to bed.

Yesterday we were travelling within the confines of civilization. Today, abruptly, we leave civilization behind. Within an hour or two there is no green to be seen anywhere. Everything is brown sandy waste. The tracks seem confusing. Sometimes at rare intervals we meet a lorry, that comes up suddenly out of nothingness.

It is very hot. What with the heat and the uneven-ness of the track and the badness of the taxi's springs, and the dust that you swallow and makes your face stiff and hard, I start a furious headache.

There is something frightening, and yet fascinating,

about this vast world denuded of vegetation. It is not flat like the desert between Damascus and Baghdad. Instead, you climb up and down. It feels a little as though you had become a grain of sand among the sand-castles you built on the beach as a child.

And then, after seven hours of heat and monotony and a lonely world—Palmyra!

That, I think, is the charm of Palmyra—its slender creamy beauty rising up fantastically in the middle of hot sand. It is lovely and fantastic and unbelievable, with all the theatrical implausibility of a dream. Courts and temples and ruined columns. . . .

I have never been able to decide what I really think of Palmyra. It has always for me the dream-like quality of that first vision. My aching head and eyes made it more than ever seem a feverish delusion! It isn't—it can't be—*real*.

But suddenly we are in the middle of people—a crowd of cheerful French tourists, laughing and talking and snapping cameras. We pull up in front of a handsome building—the Hotel.

Max warns me hurriedly: "You mustn't mind the smell. It takes a little getting used to."

It certainly does! The Hotel is charming inside, arranged with real taste and charm. But the smell of stale water in the bedroom is very strong.

"It's quite a healthy smell," Max assures me.

And the charming elderly gentleman, who is, I understand, the Hotel proprietor, says with great emphasis:

"Mauvaise odeur, *oui!* Malsain, *non!*"

So that is settled! And, anyway, I do not care. I take aspirin and drink tea and lie down on the bed. Later, I say, I will do sight-seeing—just now I care for nothing but darkness and rest.

Inwardly I feel a little dismayed. Am I going to be a bad traveller—I, who have always enjoyed motoring?

However, I wake up an hour later, feeling perfectly restored and eager to see what can be seen.

Mac, even, for once submits to being torn from his diary.

We go out sight-seeing, and spend a delightful after-noon.

When we are at the farthest point from the Hotel we run into the party of French people. They are in distress. One of the women, who is wearing (as all are) high-heeled shoes, has torn off the heel of her shoe, and is faced with the impossibility of walking back the distance to the Hotel. They have driven out to this point, it appears, in a taxi, and the taxi has now broken down. We cast an eye over it. There appears to be but one kind of taxi in this country. This vehicle is indistinguishable from ours—the same dilapidated upholstery and general air of being tied up with string. The driver, a tall, lank Syrian, is poking in a dispirited fashion into the bonnet.

He shakes his head. The French party explain all. They have arrived here by 'plane yesterday, and will leave the same way to-morrow. This taxi they have hired for the afternoon at the Hotel, and now it has broken down. What will poor Madame do? *"Impossible de marcher, n'est ce pas, avec un soulier seulement."*

We pour out condolences, and Max gallantly offers our taxi. He will return to the Hotel and bring it out here. It can make two journeys and take us all back.

The suggestion is received with acclamations and profuse thanks, and Max sets off.

I fraternise with the French ladies, and Mac retires behind an impenetrable wall of reserve. He produces a stark "Oui" or "Non" to any conversational openings, and is soon mercifully left in peace. The French ladies profess a charming interest in our journeyings.

"Ah, Madame, vous faites le camping?"

I am fascinated by the phrase. *Le camping!* It classes our adventure definitely as a sport!

How agreeable it will be, says another lady, to do *le camping*.

Yes, I say, it will be very agreeable.

The time passes; we chat and laugh. Suddenly, to my great surprise, Queen Mary comes lurching along. Max, with an angry face, is at the wheel.

I demand why he hasn't brought the taxi?

"Because," says Max furiously, "the taxi is *here*." And he points a dramatic finger at the obdurate car, into which the lank Syrian is still optimistically peering.

There is a chorus of surprised exclamations, and I realize why the car has looked so familiar! "But," cries the French lady, "this is the car we hired at the Hotel." Nevertheless, Max explains, it is *our* taxi.

Explanations with Aristide have been painful. Neither side has appreciated the other's point of view.

"Have I not hired the taxi and you for three months?" demands Max. "And must you let it out to others behind my back in this shameful way?"

"But," says Aristide, all injured innocence, "did you not tell me that you yourself would not use it this afternoon? Naturally, then, I have the chance to make a little extra money. I arrange with a friend, and he drives this party round Palmyra. How can it injure you, since you do not want to sit in the car yourself?"

"It injures me," replies Max, "since in the first place it was not our arrangement; and in the second place the car is now in need of repair, and in all probability will not be able to proceed to-morrow!"

"As to that," says Aristide, "do not disquiet yourself. My friend and I will, if necessary, sit up all night!"

Max replies briefly that they'd better.

Sure enough, the next morning the faithful taxi awaits us in front of the door, with Aristide smiling, and still quite unconvinced of sin, at the wheel.

To-day we arrive at Der Ez Zor, on the Euphrates. It is very hot. The town smells and is not attractive. The Services Spéciaux kindly puts some rooms at our disposal, since there is no European hotel. There is an attractive view over the wide brown flow of the river. The French officer inquires tenderly after my health, and hopes I have not found motoring in the heat too much for me. "Madame Jacquot, the wife of our General, was *complètement knock out* when she arrived."

The term takes my fancy. I hope that I, in my turn, shall not be *complètement knock out* by the end of our survey!

We buy vegetables and large quantities of eggs, and with Queen Mary full to the point of breaking her springs, we set off, this time to start on the survey proper.

Busaira! Here there is a police post. It is a spot of which Max has had high hopes, since it is at the junction of the Euphrates with the Habur. Roman Circesium is on the opposite bank.

Busaira proves, however, disappointing. There are no signs of any antique settlement other than Roman, which is treated with the proper disgust. "Min ziman er Rum," says Hamoudi, shaking his head distastefully, and I echo him dutifully.

For to our point of view the Romans are hopelessly modern—children of yesterday. Our interest begins at the second millennium B.C., with the varying fortunes of the Hittites, and in particular we want to find out more about the military dynasty of Mitanni, foreign adventurers about whom little is known, but who flourished in this part of the world, and whose capital city of Washshukkanni has yet to be identified. A ruling caste of warriors, who imposed their rule on the country, and who intermarried with the Royal House of Egypt, and who were, it seems, good horsemen, since a treatise upon the care and training of horses is ascribed to a certain Kikkouli, a man of Mitanni.

And from that period backwards, of course, into the dim ages of pre-history—an age without written records, when only pots, and house plans, and amulets, ornaments, and beads, remain to give their dumb witness to the life the people lived.

Busaira, having been disappointing, we go on to Meyadin, farther south, though Max has not much hope of it. After that we will strike northward up the left bank of the Habur river.

It is at Busaira that I get my first sight of the Habur,

which has so far been only a name to me—though a name that has been repeatedly on Max's lips.

"The Habur—that's the place. Hundreds of Tells!"

He goes on: "And if we don't find what we want on the Habur, we will on the Jaghjagha!"

"What," I ask, the first time I hear the name, "is the Jaghjagha?"

The name seems to me quite fantastic!

Max says kindly that he supposes I have never heard of the Jaghjagha? A good many people haven't, he concedes.

I admit the charge and add that until he mentioned it, I had not even heard of the Habur. That does surprise him.

"Didn't you know," says Max, marvelling at my shocking ignorance, "that Tell Halaf is on the Habur?"

His voice is lowered in reverence as he speaks of that famous site of prehistoric pottery.

I shake my head and forbear to point out that if I had not happened to marry him I should probably never have heard of Tell Halaf!

I may say that explaining the places where we dig to people is always fraught with a good deal of difficulty.

My first answer is usually one word—"Syria."

"Oh!" says the average inquirer, already slightly taken aback. A frown forms on his or her forehead. "Yes, of course—Syria. . . ." Biblical memories stir. "Let me see, that's Palestine, isn't it?"

"It's next to Palestine," I say encouragingly. "You know—farther up the coast."

This doesn't really help, because Palestine, being usually connected with Bible history and the lessons on Sunday rather than a geographical situation, has associations that are purely literary and religious.

"I can't quite place it." The frown deepens. "Whereabouts do you dig—I mean near what *town?*"

"Not near any town. Near the Turkish and Iraq border."

A hopeless expression then cames across the friend's face.

"But surely you must be near *some* town!"

"Alep," I say, "is about two hundred miles away."

They sigh and give it up. Then, brightening, they ask what we eat. "Just dates, I suppose?"

When I say that we have mutton, chickens, eggs, rice, French beans, aubergines, cucumbers, oranges in season and bananas, they look at me reproachfully. "I don't call that *roughing* it," they say.

At Meyadin *le camping* begins.

A chair is set up for me, and I sit in it grandly in the midst of a large courtyard, or khan; whilst Max, Mac, Aristide, Hamoudi, and Abdullah struggle to set up our tents.

There is no doubt that I have the best of it. It is a richly entertaining spectacle. There is a strong desert wind blowing which does not help, and everybody is raw to the job. Appeals to the compassion and mercy of God rise from Abdullah, demands to be assisted by the saints from Armenian Aristide, wild yells of encouragement and laughter are offered by Hamoudi, furious imprecations come from Max. Only Mac toils in silence, though even he occasionally mutters a quiet word under his breath.

At last all is ready. The tents look a little drunken, a little out of the true, but they have arisen. We all unite in cursing the cook, who, instead of starting to prepare a meal, has been enjoying the spectacle. However, we have some useful tins, which are opened, tea is made, and now, as the sun sinks and the wind drops and a sudden chill arises, we go to bed. It is my first experience of struggling into a sleeping-bag. It takes the united efforts of Max and myself, but, once inside, I am enchantingly comfortable. I always take abroad with me one really good soft down pillow —to me it makes all the difference between comfort and misery.

I say happily to Max: "I think I like sleeping in a tent!"

Then a sudden thought occurs to me.

"You don't think, do you, that rats or mice or something will run across me in the night?"

"Sure to," says Max cheerfully and sleepily.

I am digesting this thought when sleep overtakes me, and I wake to find it is five A.M.—sunrise, and time to get up and start a new day.

The mounds in the immediate neighborhood of Meyadin prove unattractive.

"Roman!" murmurs Max disgustedly. It is his last word of contempt. Stifling any lingering feeling I may have that the Romans were an interesting people, I echo his tone, and say "Roman," and cast down a fragment of the despised pottery. "Min Ziman . . . er Rum," says Hamoudi.

In the afternoon we go to visit the American dig at Doura. It is a pleasant visit, and they are charming to us. Yet I find my interest in the finds flagging, and an increasing difficulty in listening or in taking part in the conversation.

Their account of their original difficulties in getting workmen is amusing.

Working for wages in this out-of-the-way part of the world is an idea that is entirely new. The expedition found itself faced with blank refusal or non-comprehension. In despair they appealed to the French military authorities. The response was prompt and efficient. The French arrested two hundred, or whatever the number needed was, and delivered them at work. The prisoners were amiable, in the highest good humour, and seemed to enjoy the work. They were told to return on the following day, but did not turn up. Again the French were asked to help, and once again they arrested the workmen. Again the men worked with evident satisfaction. But yet again they failed to turn up, and once again military arrest was resorted to.

Finally the matter was elucidated.

"Do you not like working for us?"

"Yes, indeed, why not? We have nothing to do at home."

"Then why do you not come every day?"

"We wish to come, but naturally we have to wait for the *'asker* (soldiers) to fetch us. I can tell you, we were very indignant when they did not come to fetch us! It is their duty!"

"But we want you to work for us without the *'asker* fetching you!"

"That is a very curious idea!"

At the end of a week they were paid, and that finally set the seal on their bewilderment.

Truly, they said, they could not understand the ways of foreigners!

"The French *'asker* are in command here. Naturally, it is their right to fetch us, and put us in prison or send us to dig up the ground for you. But why do you give us money? What is the money *for*? It does not make sense!"

However, in the end the strange customs of the West were accepted, howbeit with head shakings and mutterings. Once a week money was paid them. But a vague grudge against the *'asker* remained. The *'asker's* job was to fetch them every day!

Whether true or not, this makes a good story! I only wish I could feel more intelligent. What is the matter with me? When I get back to camp my head is swimming. I take my temperature, and find that it is a hundred and two! Also, I have a pain in my middle, and feel extremely sick. I am very glad to crawl into my flea-bag and go to sleep, spurning the thought of dinner.

Max looks worried this morning and asks me how I feel. I groan and say: "Like death!" He looks more worried. He asks me if I think I am really ill?

I reassure him on that point. I have what is called in

Egypt a Gippy tummy and in Baghdad a Baghdad
tummy. It is not a very amusing complaint to have
when you are right out in the desert. Max cannot leave
me behind alone, and in any case the inside of the
tent in the day-time registers about 130! The survey
must go on. I sit huddled up in the car, swaying about
in a feverish dream. When we reach a mound, I get
out and lie down in what shade the height of Queen
Mary affords, whilst Max and Mac tramp over the
mound, examining it.

Frankly, the next four days are sheer unmitigated
hell! One of Hamoudi's stories seems particularly appo-
site—that of a Sultan's lovely wife, whom he carried
off, and who bewailed to Allah night and day that she
had no companions and was alone in the desert. "And
at last Allah, weary of her moanings, sent her companions. He sent her the flies!"

I feel particularly venomous towards the lovely lady
for incurring the wrath of Allah! All day long flies
settling in clouds make it impossible to rest.

I regret bitterly that I have ever come on this expedition, but just manage not to say so.

After four days, with nothing but weak tea without
milk, I suddenly revive. Life is good again. I eat a
colossal meal of rice and stew of vegetables swimming
in grease. It seems the most delicious thing I have
ever tasted!

After it, we climb up the mound at which we have
pitched our camp—Tell Suwar, on the left bank of the
Habur. Here there is nothing—no village, no habita-
tion of any kind, not even any Beduin tents.

There is a moon above, and below us the Habur
winds in a great S-shaped curve. The night air smells
sweet after the heat of the day.

I say: "What a lovely mound! Can't we dig here?"

Max shakes his head sadly and pronounces the word
of doom.

"Roman."

"What a pity. It's such a lovely spot."

"I told you," said Max, "that the Habur was the place! Tells all along it on either side."

I have taken no interest in Tells for several days, but I am glad to find I have not missed much.

"Are you sure there isn't any of the stuff you want here?" I ask wistfully. I have taken a fancy to Tell Suwar.

"Yes, of course there is, but it's underneath. We'd have to dig right down through the Roman stuff. We can do better than that."

I sigh and murmur: "It's so still here and so peaceful—not a soul in sight."

At that moment a very old man appears from nowhere at all.

Where has he come from? He walks up the side of the mound slowly, without haste. He has a long white beard and ineffable dignity.

He salutes Max politely. "How is your comfort?" "Well. And yours?" "Well." "Praise God!" "Praise God!"

He sits down beside us. There is a long silence—that courteous silence of good manners that is so restful after Western haste.

Finally the old man inquires Max's name. Max tells it him. He considers it.

"Milwan," he repeats. "Milwan . . . How light! How bright! How beautiful!"

He sits with us a little longer. Then, as quietly as he has come, he leaves us. We never see him again.

Restored to health, I now really begin to enjoy myself. We start every morning at early dawn, examining each mound as we come to it, walking round and round it, picking up any sherds of pottery. Then we compare results on the top, and Max keeps such specimens as are useful, putting them in a little linen bag and labelling them.

There is great competition between us as to who gets the prize find of the day.

I begin to understand why archaeologists have a habit of walking with eyes downcast to the ground. Soon, I feel, I myself shall forget to look around me, or out to the horizon. I shall walk looking down at my feet as though there only any interest lies.

I am struck as often before by the fundamental difference of race. Nothing could differ more widely than the attitude of our two chauffeurs to money. Abdullah lets hardly a day pass without clamouring for an advance of salary. If he had had his way we would have had the entire amount in advance, and it would, I rather imagine, have been dissipated before a week was out. With Arab prodigality Abdullah would have splashed it about in the coffee-house. He would have cut a figure! He would have "made a reputation for himself."

Aristide, the Armenian, has displayed the greatest reluctance to have a penny for his salary paid him. "You will keep it for me, Khwaja, until the journey is finished. If I want money for some little expense I will come to you." So far he has demanded only fourpence of his salary—to purchase a pair of socks!

His chin is now adorned by a sprouting beard, which makes him look quite a Biblical figure. It is cheaper, he explains, not to shave. One saves the money one might have to spend on a razor blade. And it does not matter here in the desert.

At the end of the trip Abdullah will be penniless once more, and will doubtless be again adorning the water-front of Beyrout, waiting with Arab fatalism for the goodness of God to provide him with another job. Aristide will have the money he has earned untouched.

"And what will you do with it?" Max asks him.

"It will go towards buying a better taxi," replies Aristide.

"And when you have a better taxi?"

"Then I shall earn more and have two taxis."

I can quite easily foresee returning to Syria in twenty

years' time, and finding Aristide the immensely rich owner of a large garage, and probably living in a big house in Beyrout. And even then, I dare say, he will avoid shaving in the desert because it saves the price of a razor blade.

And yet Aristide has not been brought up by his own people. One day, as we pass some Beduin, he is hailed by them, and cries back to them, waving and shouting affectionately.

"That," he explains, "is the Anaizah tribe, of whom I am one."

"How is that?" Max asks.

And then Aristide, in his gentle, happy voice, with his quite cheerful smile, tells the story. The story of a little boy of seven, who with his family and other Armenian families was thrown by the Turks alive into a deep pit. Tar was poured on them and set alight. His father and mother and two brothers and sisters were all burnt alive. But he, who was below them all, was still alive when the Turks left, and he was found later by some of the Anaizah Arabs. They took the little boy with them and adopted him into the Anaizah tribe. He was brought up as an Arab, wandering with them over their pastures. But when he was eighteen he went into Mosul, and there demanded that papers be given him to show his nationality. He was an Armenian, not an Arab! Yet the blood brotherhood still holds, and to members of the Anaizah he still is one of them.

Hamoudi and Max are very gay together. They laugh and sing and cap stories. Sometimes I ask for a translation when the mirth is particularly hilarious. There are moments when I feel envious of the fun they are having. Mac is still separated from me by an impassable barrier. We sit together at the back of the car in silence. Any remark I make is considered gravely on its merits by Mac and disposed of accordingly. Never have I felt less of a social success! Mac, on the

other hand, seems quite happy. There is about him a
beautiful self-sufficiency which I cannot but admire.

Nevertheless, when, encased in my sleeping-bag at
night in the privacy of our tent. I hold forth to Max
on the incidents of the day, I strenuously maintain that
Mac is *not* quite human!

When Mac does advance an original comment it is
usually of a damping nature. Adverse criticism seems
to afford him a definite gloomy satisfaction.

Am perplexed to-day by the growing uncertainty of
my walking powers. In some curious way my feet
don't seem to match. I am puzzled by a decided list to
port. Is it, I wonder fearfully, the first symptoms of
some tropical disease?

I ask Max if he has noticed that I can't walk straight.

"But you never drink," he replies. "Heaven knows,"
he adds reproachfully, "I've tried hard enough with
you."

This introduces a second and controversial subject.
Everyone struggles through life with some unfortunate
disability. Mine is to be unable to appreciate either
alcohol or tobacco.

If I could only bring myself to disapprove of these
essential products my self-respect would be saved. But,
on the contrary, I look with envy at self-possessed
women flipping cigarette ash here, there, and everywhere, and creep miserably round the room at cocktail parties finding a place to hide my untasted glass.

Perseverance has not availed. For six months I
religiously smoked a cigarette after lunch and after
dinner, choking a little, biting fragments of tobacco,
and blinking as the ascending smoke pricked my eye-
lid. Soon, I told myself, I should learn to like smoking.
I did not learn to like it, and my performance was
criticized severely as being inartistic and painful to
watch. I accepted defeat.

When I married Max we enjoyed the pleasures of the
table in perfect harmony, eating wisely but much too

well. He was distressed to find that my appreciation of good drink—or, indeed, of any drink, was *nil*. He set to work to educate me, trying me perseveringly with clarets, burgundies, sauternes, graves, and, more desperately, with tokay, vodka, and absinthe! In the end he acknowledged defeat. My only reaction was that some tasted worse than others! With a weary sigh, Max contemplated a life in which he should be for ever condemned to the battle of obtaining water for me in a restaurant! It has added, he says, years to his life.

Hence his remarks when I enlist his sympathy for my drunken progress.

"I seem," I explain, "to be always falling over to the left."

Max says it is probably one of these very rare tropical diseases that are distinguished by just being called by somebody's name. Stephenson's disease—or Hartley's. The sort of thing, he goes on cheerfully, which will probably end with your toes falling off one by one.

I contemplate this pleasing prospect. Then it occurs to me to look at my shoes. The mystery is at once explained. The outer sole of my left foot and the inner sole of the right foot are worn right down. As I stare at them the full solution dawns on me. Since leaving Der-ez-Zor I have walked round about fifty mounds, at different levels, on the side of a steep slope, but always with the hill on my left. All that is needed is to go into reverse, and go round mounds to the right instead of the left. In due course my shoes will then be worn even.

Today we arrive at Tell Ajaja, the former Arban, a large and important Tell.

The main track from Der-ez-Zor joins in near here, so we feel now we are practically on a main road. Actually we pass three cars, all going hell-for-leather in the direction of Der-ez-Zor!

Small clusters of mud houses adorn the Tell, and various people pass the time of day with us upon the big mound. This is practically civilization. Tomorrow we shall arrive at Hasetshe, the junction of the Habur and the Jaghjagha. Then we shall be *in* civilization. It is a French military post, and an important town in this part of the world. There I shall have my first sight of the legendary and long-promised Jaghjagha river! I feel quite excited.

Our arrival at Hasetshe is full of excitement. It is an unattractive place, with streets and a few shops and a post office. We pay two ceremonious visits—one to the Military and one to the Post Office.

The French Lieutenant is most kind and helpful. He offers us hospitality, but we assure him that our tents are quite comfortable where we have pitched them by the river bank. We accept, however, an invitation to dinner on the following day. The Post Office, where we go for letters, is a longer business. The Postmaster is out, and everything is consequently locked up. However, a small boy goes in search of him, and in due course (half an hour!) he arrives, full of urbanity, bids us welcome to Hasetshe, orders coffee for us, and only after a prolonged exchange of compliments comes to the business in hand—letters.

"But there is no hurry," he says, beaming. "Come again tomorrow. I shall be delighted to entertain you."

"Tomorrow," Max says, "we have work to do. We should like our letters tonight."

Ah, but here is the coffee! We sit and sip. At long last, after polite exhortations, the Postmaster unlocks his private office and starts to search. In the generosity of his heart he urges on us additional letters addressed to other Europeans. "You had better have these," he says. "They have been here six months. No one has come for them. Yes, yes, surely they will be for you."

Politely but firmly, we refuse the correspondence of Mr. Johnson, M. Mavrogordata, and Mr. Pye. The Postmaster is disappointed.

"So few?" he says. "But come, will you not have this large one here?"

But we insist on sticking strictly to those letters and papers that bear our own names. A money order has come, as arranged, and Max now goes into the question of cashing it. This, it seems, is incredibly complicated. The Postmaster has never seen a money order before, we gather, and is very properly suspicious of it. He calls in two assistants, and the question is debated thoroughly, though with great good humor. Here is something entirely novel and delightful on which everyone can have a different opinion.

The matter is finally settled and various forms signed, when the discovery is made that there is no actual cash in the Post Office! This, the Postmaster says, can be remedied on the morrow. He will send out and collect it from the Bazaar.

We leave the Post Office somewhat exhausted, and walk back to the spot by the river which we have chosen—a little way from the dust and dirt of Hasetshe. A sad spectacle greets us. 'Isa, the cook, is sitting by the cooking-tent, his head in his hands, weeping bitterly.

What has happened?

Alas, he replies, he is disgraced. Little boys have collected round to jeer at him. His honor has gone! In a moment of inattention dogs have devoured the dinner he had prepared. There is nothing left, nothing at all but some rice.

Gloomily we eat plain rice, whilst Hamoudi, Aristide, and Abdullah reiterate to the wretched 'Isa that the principal duty of a cook is never to let his attention wander from the dinner he is cooking until the moment when that dinner is safely set before those for whom it is destined.

'Isa says that he feels he is unequal to the strain of being a cook. He has never been one before ("That explains a good deal!" says Max), and would prefer to go into a garage. Will Max give him a recommendation as a first-class driver?

Max says certainly not, as he has never seen him drive.

"But," says 'Isa, "I have wound the handle of Big Mary on a cold morning. You have seen that?"

Max admits that he has seen that.

"Then," says 'Isa, "you can recommend me!"

III

THE HABUR AND
THE JAGHJAGHA

THESE AUTUMN DAYS are some of the most perfect I have ever known. We get up early, soon after sunrise, drink hot tea, and eat eggs and start off. It is cold then, and I wear two jerseys and a big woolly coat. The light is lovely—a very faint soft rose softens the browns and greys. From the top of a mound one looks out over an apparently deserted world. Mounds rise everywhere—one can see perhaps sixty if one counts. Sixty ancient settlements, that is to say. Here, where nowadays only the tribesmen move with their brown tents, was once a busy part of the world. Here, some five thousand years ago, was *the* busy part of the world. Here were the beginnings of civilization, and here, picked up by me, this broken fragment of a clay pot, hand made, with a design of dots and cross-hatching in black paint, is the forerunner of the Woolworth cup out of which this very morning I have drunk my tea. . . .

I sort through the collection of sherds which are bulging the pockets of my coat (I have already had to mend the lining twice), throwing away duplicate

types, and see what I can offer in competition with
Mac and Hamoudi to the Master for judgment.

Now then, what have I got?

A thickish grey ware, part of the rim of a pot (valuable as showing shape), some coarse red stuff, two
fragments of painted pots, hand-made and one with the
dot design (the oldest Tell Halaf!), a flint knife, part
of the base of a thin grey pot, several other nondescript bits of painted pottery, a little bit of obsidian.

Max makes his selection, flinging most pieces ruthlessly away, uttering appreciative grunts at others.
Hamoudi has the clay wheel of a chariot, and Mac
has a fragment of incised ware and a portion of a
figurine.

Gathering the united collection together, Max sweeps
them into a little linen bag, ties it carefully up, and
labels it as usual with the name of the Tell on which
it was found. This particular Tell is not marked on the
map. It is christened Tel Mak in honor of Macartney
who has had the first find.

So far as Mac's countenance can express anything at
all, it seems to express faint gratification.

We run down the side of the Tell and climb into the
car. I peel off a jersey. The sun is getting hot.

We visit two more small Tells, and at the third,
which overlooks the Habur, we have lunch—hard-
boiled eggs, a tin of bully beef, oranges, and extremely
stale bread. Aristide makes tea on the primus. It is
very hot now, and the shadows and colors have gone.
All is a uniform soft pale buff.

Max says it is lucky we are doing the survey now
and not in spring. I ask why? And he says, because
it would be far more difficult to fine sherds when there
is vegetation everywhere. All this, he says, will be green
in the spring. It is, he says, the fertile Steppe. I say
admiringly that that is a very grand way of putting
it. Max says, well it *is* the fertile Steppe!

Today we take Mary up the right bank of the Habur
to Tell Halaf, visiting Tell Ruman (sinister name, but

actually not noticeably Roman) and Tell Juma on the way.

All the Tells in this region have possibilities, unlike the ones farther south. Sherds of pottery of the second and third millennium are frequent and Roman remains are scanty. There is early prehistoric painted hand-made pottery as well. The difficulty will be to choose between so many Tells. Max repeats again and again with jubilation and a complete lack of originality that this is undoubtedly the place!

Our visit to Tell Halaf has something of the reverence of a pilgrimage to a shrine! Tell Halaf is a name that has been so constantly dinned into my ears for the last few years that I can hardly believe I am actually going to see the actual spot. A very lovely spot it is, with the Habur winding round the base of it.

I recall a visit we paid to Baron von Oppenheim in Berlin when he took us to the Museum of his finds. Max and he talked excitedly for (I think) five solid hours. There was nowhere to sit down. My interest, at first acute, flagged, and finally died down completely. With lack-lustre eyes I examined the various extremely ugly statues which had come from Tell Halaf, and which in the Baron's view were contemporary with the extremely interesting pottery. Max was endeavoring to differ politely on this point without contradicting him flatly. To my dazed glance all the statues seemed strangely alike. It was only after a little while that I made the discovery that they *were* alike, since all but one were plaster reproductions.

Baron von Oppenheim stopped in his eager dissertation to say lovingly: "Ah, my beautiful Venus," and stroke the figure affectionately. Then he plunged back into discussion, and I wished sadly that I could, in the old nursery phrase, cut off my feet and turn up the ends!

We have many local conversations on the various mounds approaching Tell Halaf. All hereabouts are various legends of El Baron—mainly the incredible

sums he paid out in gold. Time has exaggerated the
amount of gold. Even the German government, one
feels, cannot have poured out the streams of precious
metal in the way tradition has it! Everywhere north of
Hasetshe are small villages and signs of cultivation.
Since the arrival of the French and the departure of
the Turkish rule, the country is being occupied again
for the first time since Roman days.

We get home late. The weather is changing, a wind
starts blowing, and it is very unpleasant, dust and sand
flying in one's face and making one's eyes smart. We
have a pleasant dinner with the French, though it has
been a difficult business smartening oneself up, or
rather, I should say, cleaning oneself up, since a clean
blouse for myself and clean shirts for the men is all
one can do! We have an excellent dinner and spend a
very pleasant evening. We return through driving rain
to our tents. An unquiet night, with dogs howling and
the tents flapping and straining in the wind.

Forsaking the Habur for the time being, we make
an excursion today on the Jaghjagha. An immense
mound quite near at hand has excited my interest,
until I discover that it is an extinct volcano—the
Kawkab.

Our particular objective is one Tell Hamidi, of
which we have heard good accounts, but it is difficult
to reach, as there is no direct track. It means taking a
line across country and the crossing of innumerable
little ditches and wadis. Hamoudi is in great spirits
this morning. Mac is quietly gloomy, and opines that
we shall never get to the mound.

It takes us seven hours of motoring—a very tiring
seven hours, with the car sticking more than once and
having to be dug out.

Hamoudi surpasses himself on these occasions. He
always considers a car as a kind of inferior though
swifter horse. In any moment of uncertainty with a
wadi ahead, Hamoudi's voice rises excitedly, giving
frenzied orders to Aristide.

"Quickly—quickly! Give the machine no time to refuse! Rush at it! Rush at it!"

His disgust when Max stops the car and walks ahead to examine the difficulty is extreme. He shakes his head in utter dissatisfaction.

Not so, he seems to say, should you treat a high-mettled and nervous car! Give it no time to reflect and all will be well.

After detours, checks, and the taking on of local guides, we do at last reach the goal. Very beautiful Tell Hamidi looks in the afternoon sun, and it is with a sense of achievement that the car drives proudly up the gentle incline to its summit where we look down on a marsh teeming with wild duck.

Mac is sufficiently moved to utter a remark.

"Ah," he says in a tone of gloomy satisfaction, "stagnant water, I see!"

It is hereafter to be his nickname!

Life now becomes hurried and hectic. Examination of Tells is daily more zealous. For the final selection three things are essential. First, it must be sufficiently near a village or villages to get a supply of labor. Secondly, there must be a water supply—that is to say, it must be near the Jaghjagha or the Habur, or else there must be well-water that is not too brackish. Thirdly, it must give indications of having the right stuff in it. All digging is a gamble—among seventy Tells all occupied at the same period, who is to say which one holds a building, or a deposit of tablets, or a collection of objects of special interest? A small Tell offers as good prospects as a large Tell, since the more important towns are the more likely to have been looted and destroyed in the far-distant past. Luck is the predominant factor. How often has a site been painstakingly and correctly dug, season after season, with interesting but not spectacular results, and then a shift of a few feet, and suddenly a unique find comes to light. The one real consolation is that whichever Tell we select, we are bound to find *something*.

We have made a day's excursion on the opposite
bank of the Habur to Tell Halaf again, and we have
done two days on the Jaghjagha—a much overrated
river, from the point of view of appearance—a brown
muddy stream between high banks—and have marked
down one Tell—Tell Brak—as highly promising. It is
a large mound, with traces of several periods of occupation, from early prehistoric to Assyrian times. It is
about two miles from the Jaghjagha, where there is an
Armenian settlement, and there are other villages
scattered around not very far away. It is about an
hour's drive from Hasetshe, which will be convenient
for supplies. As a drawback, there is no water at the
Tell itself, though possibly a well could be dug there.
Tell Brak goes down as a possibility.

Today we take the main track from Hasetshe north-
west to Kamichlie—another French military post, and
the frontier town between Syria and Turkey. The
track runs about midway between the Habur and the
Jaghjagha for some distance, and finally rejoins
the Jaghjagha at Kamichlie.

Since to examine all the Tells on the way and return
to Hasetshe that night would be impossible, we decide
to stay the night in Kamichlie and return the following day.

Opinions as to accommodation vary. According to
the French Lieutenant, the so-called Hotel at Kamichlie
is impossible, but impossible! *"C'este infecte, Madame!"* According to Hamoudi and Aristide it is a
fine Hotel, quite European, with *beds!* Indeed, quite
first-class!

Stifling an inner conviction that the French Lieutenant will be proved right, we set off.

The weather has cleared again after two days of
drizzling rain. It is hoped that bad weather will not
really set in before December. There are two deep
wadis between Hasetshe and Kamichlie, and if they
fill with water the road will be cut for some days. There
is only a little water in them today, and we switchback
down and up again without much difficulty—that is

to say, we in Aristide's taxi do so. Abdullah, as is his invariable custom, sweeps down in top gear, and endeavors to come up the other side in the same. He then tries to change down into second while the car is at a standstill. The engine protests and stops, and Abdullah glides gently back to the bottom of the wadi, his back wheels in mud and water. We all get out and make our contribution to the situation.

Max curses Abdullah for a damned fool, and why can't he do as he has been told a hundred times? Hamoudi upbraids him for lack of speed: "Faster, faster! You showed too much caution. Give the car no time to reflect. It would not then have refused." Aristides cries gaily: "Inshallah, we shall be out of here in ten minutes!" Mac breaks his silence to utter one of his usual depressing statements. "About the worst place he *could* get stuck. Look at the angle! We shan't get out of that for a long time." Abdullah raises his hands to heaven and utters a shrill vindication of his methods. "With such a fine car as this we might easily have sailed up in third, and then there would have been no need to change down at all, and in that way petrol would have been saved! I do everything in order to please you!"

The chorus of lamentations gives way to practical proceedings. The boards, pickaxes, and other equipment always carried for these predicaments are unshipped. Max pushes Abdullah aside and takes his place at Mary's wheel; the boards are placed in position; Mac, Hamoudi, Aristide, and Abdullah take their places ready to shove. Since Khatuns toil not in the East (an excellent idea!), I take my stand upon the bank, prepared to utter cries of encouragement and helpful advice. Max starts the engine and revs it up; clouds of blue smoke arise from the exhaust, practically asphyxiating the shovers; Max puts the car into gear and eases out the clutch; there is a terrific roar; wheels spin; the blue haze grows; out of it are heard shrill cries that Allah is excessively merciful, Mary advances a couple of feet, the clamor increases, Allah *is* very merciful. . . .

Alas, Allah is not merciful enough! The wheels lose grip and Mary sinks back. Renewed disposal of boards, renewed efforts, shouting, fountains of mud, and blue fumes. Very nearly this time!

Just a little more power is needed. The tow-rope is attached to Mary's nose and fastened to the back of the taxi. Aristide takes his place at the taxi's wheel. Everyone gets into position. Aristide displays too much zeal and lets in the clutch too soon. The tow-rope snaps. Fresh start. I am given the post of synchronizer. When I signal with the handkerchief, Aristide is to start.

Once more the maneuvers begin. Hamoudi, Abdullah and Mac prepare to shove, the two former uttering encouraging cries to the car well beforehand. Once again Max starts off. Once more fountains of mud and water arise mingled with blue smoke; the engine pants and races; the wheels start moving; I drop the handkerchief; Aristide utters a wild high scream, crosses himself, shouts Allah Kerim, and crashes in his gear. Slowly, groaning, Mary quavers forward; the tow-rope tightens; she hesitates; her back wheels spin; Max zigzags wildly; she recovers, and zigzagging to and fro up the steep bank, up she comes!

Two figures, completely drowned in mud, rush up after her, yelling happily. A third figure, also mud-stained, walks up soberly—the imperturbable Mac. He shows no signs of either discomposure or of exultation.

I look at my watch and say: "A quarter of an hour. Not too bad." Mac replies calmly: "The next wadi will probably be worse."

Decidedly, Mac is not human!

We proceed. Homoudi enlivens the road with snatches of song. He and Max are having a gay time together in front. Mac and I sit in silence behind. I am by this time reduced to gibbering idiocy when I attempt conversation. Mac bears with my idiotic remarks patiently and politely as always, according them a deliber-

ate attention they do not deserve, and replies to them
with one or other of his formulas: "Indeed?" or gently
and reprovingly, "Surely that is not so?"

Presently we arrive at the second wadi. We halt;
Max takes Abdullah's place in Mary. Aristide goes
through first without mishap. Max follows, going down
in second and changing to first as he starts up out of
the water. Mary arrives, lurching triumphantly.

"You see?" says Max to Abdullah.

Abdullah puts on his most camel-like expression.

"She would have done it this time in third," he says.
"You did not need to change."

Max tells him again that he is a damned fool, and
adds that at any rate he is to do as he is told in
future. Abdullah replies cheerfully that he always does
everything for the best.

Max abandons the argument and we proceed.

Tells are plentiful. I begin to wonder whether the
moment has not come to resume my anti-clockwise
progress round them.

We arrive at a Tell named Chagar Bazar. Dogs and
children rush out from the small cluster of houses.
Presently a striking figure is seen in flowing white robes
and a brilliant green turban. It is the local Sheikh. He
greets us with the utmost bonhomie. Max disappears
with him into the largest mud house. After a pause of
some moments the Sheikh reappears and yells: "Engineer! Where is the engineer?" Hamoudi explains that
this summons is intended for Mac. Mac goes forward.

"Ha," cries the Sheikh, "here is *leben!*" He produces a bowl of the local sour milk. "How do you
like your *leben,* engineer, thick or thin?" Mac, who is
very fond of *leben,* nods towards the water-jug the
Sheikh is holding. I see Max endeavoring to negative
the suggestion. Too late; the water is added to the
leben, and Mac drinks it off with something like relish.

"I tried to warn you," says Max later. "That water
was practically thin black mud!"

The finds on Chagar Bazar are good. . . . There is a
village, wells, other villages adjacent, and a kindly

disposed, though no doubt rapacious, Sheikh. It is put down as a possible, and we go on.

A few detours over marshy ground to reach certain Tells near the Jaghjagha at the end of the day delay us, and it is quite late when we arrive at last at Kamichlie.

With the utmost enthusiasm Aristide pulls up the car with a jerk before the first-class Hotel.

"See," he says, "is it not handsome? It is built of *stone!*"

We forbear to say that the inside of hotels is more important than the outside. Anyway, here *is* the Hotel, and whatever it is like, it has to do.

We enter, climb up a long dingy stair, and arrive in a restaurant with marble-topped tables, where there is a thick smell of paraffin, garlic, and smoke.

Max enters into negotiations with the Proprietor.

Certainly this is a Hotel. It is a Hotel with beds—real beds! He flings open the door of a room, in which four people, already asleep on beds, prove the truth of his words. There are two unoccupied beds in the room.

"There you are," he says; "and this animal here"—he kicks the nearest sleeper—"can be turned out! He is only my horse-boy."

Max makes the unreasonable request that we would like a room to ourselves. The Proprietor is doubtful. That, he says, will be enormously expensive.

Max says recklessly that he does not mind if it *is* expensive. How expensive, he asks, will it be?

The Proprietor hesitates, scratches his ear, sizes up our appearance (which, owing to mud, is not very plutocratic), and finally hazards the opinion that it will cost at least a pound for the four of us.

To his stupefaction Max agrees without bargaining.

Immediately all is activity and enthusiasm. Sleepers are aroused, servants are called. We sit down at one of the marble tables and order the best meal the house can provide.

Hamoudi charges himself with the supervision of the

sleeping accommodation. He returns some quarter of
an hour later all smiles. One room is to be at the
disposal of Max and myself. He and Mac will share
the other. Also, "and for the good of your reputation,"
as he puts it, he has agreed to an additional charge
of five francs for clean sheets!

The food comes; it is greasy, but hot and savoury.
We eat heartily, and without more ado retire and fall
on to the clean-sheeted beds. As I fall asleep, the
possible question of "bugs" just stirs in my mind. Max
gives it as his opinion that we are safe from bugs. This
place is only recently built, and the beds are new ones
of iron.

The fumes of smoke, garlic, and paraffin seep in
through the restaurant next door, and there is the high
chatter of Arab voices. But nothing can keep us from
sleep. We sleep.

We awake, unbitten. It is later than we thought.
Once again we have a full day before us. Max throws
open the bedroom door and blenches slightly. The
restaurant is full of the dispossessed sleepers from the
two bedrooms. They lie about among the tables—there
are at least a score of them. The atmosphere is very
thick. Tea and eggs are brought to us, and we set off
once more. Hamoudi says sadly to Max that he has
talked long and earnestly to the Khwaja Macartney
last night, but alas, not even now, after two months
does the Khwaja Mac understand a word of Arabic!

Max asks Mac how he is getting on with Van Ess's
spoken Arabic. Mac replies that he seems to have
mislaid it.

After doing some shopping in Kamichlie, we take
the road of Amuda. This is an important road—
almost, one might say, a real road instead of a track.
It runs parallel with the railway line, on the other
side of which is Turkey.

Its surface is appalling—continual ruts and holes.
We are all shaken to bits, but there is no doubt that
one sees life on it. We pass several cars, and both
Abdullah and Aristide have to be severely cursed for

indulging in the native driver's favorite sport of trying to run down, or, at any rate, severely frighten, parties of donkeys and camels in charge of old women and boys.

"It not this track wide enough for you to pass right at the other side?" demands Max.

Abdullah turns to him excitedly.

"Am I not driving a lorry? Am I not to choose the best surface? These miserable Beduin must get out of my way, they and their wretched donkeys!"

Aristide glides softly up behind an overladen donkey, with a man and woman trudging beside it, and lets out a terrific blast of his horn. The donkey stampedes, the woman screams and rushes after it, the man shakes his fist. Aristide roars with laughter.

He in turn is cursed, but remains, as usual, serenely unrepentant.

Amuda is mainly an Armenian town, and not, may it be said, at all an attractive one. The flies there are out of all proportion, the small boys have the worst manners yet seen, everyone seems bored and yet truculent. On the whole it compares unfavorably with Kamichlie. We buy meat of a doubtful character from which flies rise in a swarm, some rather tired vegetables, and some very good freshly made bread.

Hamoudi goes off to make various inquiries. He returns as our purchases are completed, and directs us to a side road in which is a gate leading into a courtyard.

Here we are greeted by an Armenian priest—very courteous and knowing a little French. Waving his hand round the courtyard and the building at one side of it, he says that this is his house.

Yes, he would be prepared to rent it to us next spring if the "arrangements" were satisfactory. Yes, he could clear out one room, and let us have it for storing things quite soon.

Negotiations having thus been set under way, we start off for Hasetshe. There is a direct track from Amuda joining the Kamichlie road at Tell Chagar Bazar. We examine a few Tells on the way, and arrive back at our camp without incident but extremely tired.

Max asks Mac if he has suffered inconvenience from the Sheikh's filthy water. Mac replies that he has never felt better.

"I told you Mac was a find," says Max later when we are rolled up in our flea-bags. "First-class stomach! Nothing upsets him. Can eat any amount of grease and muck. And practically never opens his mouth."

"That," I say, "may be all right for *you!* You and Hamoudi never stop roaring with laughter and talking. But what about *me?*"

"I can't understand why you don't get on with him better. Do you *try?*"

"I'm always trying. He just snubs me."

Max seems to find this amusing, and chuckles a good deal.

Today sees our arrival at Amuda—our new center of activity. Mary and the taxi are parked in the Armenian priest's courtyard. A room in the house has been cleared and is at our disposal, but Hamoudi, after examination of it, recommends sleeping in the tents still! We set them up with difficulty, for there is a strong wind blowing, and it is beginning to rain. It looks as though there would be no excursions tomorrow. Twenty-four hours' rain in these parts effectually paralyzes traffic. It is fortunate that we have got a room where we can spend the day, go over our finds up to date, and where Max can write his report of the proceedings up to date.

Mac and I unload and arrange things in the room— folding-table, deck-chairs, lamps, etc. The others go off into the town to make necessary purchases.

Outside, the wind rises and the rain begins to beat down. There are broken panes in the windows and it is very cold. I look longingly at the petrol lamp.

"I wish Abdullah would come back," I say, "and we could get the heater going."

For Abdullah, devoid apparently of any intelligence,

a shocking driver, and mentally deficient in almost
every respect, is nevertheless undisputed lord of those
temperamental things—petrol lamps. He, and he alone,
can deal with their intricacies.

Mac goes over to the heater and looks at it.

The scientific principle, he says, is quite simple.
Would I like him to light it?

I say I would, and hand him a box of matches.

Mac proceeds to the task with quiet confidence.
The methylated is ignited, and so on and so forth. His
hands are deft and skillful, and he clearly knows what
he is doing.

Time passes . . . the lamp does not light. Mac
starts all over again with the methylated. . . .

After another five minutes he murmurs, more to himself than me:

"The *principle* is clear enough——"

I steal a glance at him when another five minutes
have gone by. He is getting warm. He also is looking
not nearly so superior. Scientific principle or no scientific principle, the petrol lamp is holding out on him.
He lies on the floor and wrestles with the thing.
Presently he begins to swear. . . .

A feeling that is almost affection sweeps over me.
After all, our Mac *is* human. He is defeated by a petrol
lamp!

Half an hour later Max and Abdullah return. Mac
is scarlet in the face and the petrol lamp is unlit.

"Ah, let me do that, Khwaja!" says Abdullah. He
seizes the methylated, the matches. In two minutes the
petrol lamp is flaring away, although I feel tolerably
certain that Abdullah has completely ignored any scientific principle there may be. . . .

"Well!" says Mac, inarticulate as usual, but conveying a good deal in that one word.

Later that night the wind rises to a gale, the rain
is lashing down. Aristide runs in to say he thinks the
tents are coming down. We all rush out in the rain.
It dawns on me that I am now going to see the seamy
side of *le camping*.

Valiantly Max and Mac and Aristide struggle with the big tent. Mac clings to the pole.

Suddenly there is a snap, the pole breaks, Mac goes down headlong into thick slimy mud.

He struggles up, completely unrecognizable. His voice rises in completely natural tones:

"D—— and ——— the ——— ——— ———
thing," yells Mac at last, becoming wholly human.

From that night onward Mac is one of us!

The bad weather passes, but for a day the tracks are too wet for motoring. We venture out cautiously to Tells near at hand. A possibility is Tell Hamdun—a large Tell not far from Amuda and set right on the frontier, the railway actually passing through a portion of it, so that a slice of it is in Turkey.

We are here one morning, and have brought a couple of men with us to cut a trench in the side of the Tell. The place where they are digging is cold, and I go round to the opposite side of the Tell out of the wind. The days are definitely autumnal now, and I sit on the side of the Tell huddled down in my coat.

Suddenly, out of nowhere, as usual, a horseman comes cantering up the mound. He reins his horse and shouts to me, addressing me fluently in Arabic. I understand nothing beyond the greeting, which I return politely, and say that the Khwaja is the other side of the mound. He looks puzzled, asks me another question, then suddenly throws back his head and roars with laughter.

"Ah, it is a Khatūn!" he cries. "What a mistake! It is a Khatūn to whom I speak!" and he canters round to the other side of the mound, intensely amused at the solecism he has committed in not having recognized a female at first sight!

The best days are over. Now often there are overcast skies. We have finished examining Tells. The moment has come to decide where the spades are to go in next spring.

Three Tells compete for the honor of our attention
—Tell Hamdun, which is geographically in an interesting sector, our first selection, Tell Chagar Bazar; and
a third, Tell Mozan. This is much the largest of the
three, and a lot depends on whether there will be
much Roman deposit to dig through.

Soundings must be made at all three mounds. We
make a start with Tell Mozan. There is a village there,
and with Hamoudi as ambassador we try and obtain
workmen. The men are doubtful and suspicious.

"We do not need money," they say. "It has been a
good harvest."

For this is a simple, and, I think, consequently a
happy part of the world. Food is the only consideration. If the harvest is good, you are rich. For the rest
of the year there is leisure and plenty, until the time
comes to plough and sow once more.

"A little extra money," says Hamoudi, like the serpent of Eden, "is always welcome."

They answer simply: "But what can we buy with it?
We have enough food until the harvest comes again."

And here, alas! the eternal Eve plays her part. Astute
Hamoudi baits his hook. They can buy ornaments for
their wives.

The wives nod their heads. This digging, they say,
is a good thing!

Reluctantly the men consider the idea. There is
another thing to be taken into account—Dignity. His
dignity is very dear to an Arab. Is this a *dignified,* an
honorable thing to do?

It will only be for a few days now, explains
Hamoudi. They can reconsider before the spring.

So at last, with the doubtful expressions of those
who embark upon a new and unprecedented venture,
a dozen of the more progressive spirits step out. The
more conservative elders are shaking their white beards.

At a sign from Hamoudi, picks and spades are
unloaded from Mary and served out to the men.
Hamoudi himself takes a pick and demonstrates.

Three trial trenches are selected at different levels

of the Tell. There is a murmur of "Inshallah!" and the picks go in.

Tell Mozan has been reluctantly erased from our list of possibles. There are several levels of Roman occupation, and though the periods we want to dig are there underneath, it would take several seasons—that is to say, more time and money than we can afford.

Today we drive to our old friend Chagar Bazar. Here the arrangements for labor are quickly made. The Sheikh is a poor man, heavily in debt, like all Arab landowners. He sees in all this some very pretty profits to be made.

"All that I have is yours, brother," he says generously to Max, the light of calculation glistening in his eye. "There need be no payment for the land. Take all I have!"

Then, as Max strides up the mound, the Sheikh bends his head to Hamoudi.

"Doubtless," he suggests, "this Khwaja is immensely rich! Is he as rich as El Baron of famous memory who paid in bags of gold?"

"Nowadays," says Hamoudi, "payment is not made in gold. Nevertheless the Khwaja is extremely generous. Moreover, in all probability the Khwaja will build a house here—a house of such beauty and grandeur that it will be mentioned far and wide. What prestige will that house of the excavation not confer upon the Sheikh? All the district will say: "The foreign Khwajas chose this spot to build and dig because of its proximity to the holiness of the Sheikh, a man who has been to Mecca and whom all revere."

The idea of the house pleases the Sheikh. He looks thoughtfully up at the mound.

"I shall lose all the crops that I am about to sow on the mound there. A heavy loss—a very heavy loss!"

"But surely," says Hamoudi, "the ground would be plowed and the seed sowed before now?"

"There have been delays," says the Sheikh. "I am about to do it."

"Have you ever had any crops there? Surely not. Who would plow a hill when there are plains all round?"

The Sheikh says firmly: "The crops I shall lose will be a heavy loss. But what of it? It is a sacrifice I shall gladly make so as to please the Government. If I am ruined, what does it matter?"

And looking decidedly cheerful he goes back into his house.

An old woman comes up to Hamoudi, leading a boy of twelve by the hand.

"Has the Khwaja medicine?"

"He has some medicines—yes?"

"Will he give me medicine for my son here?"

"What is the matter with your son?"

It is hardly necessary to ask. The imbecile face is only too clear.

"He has not his proper senses."

Hamoudi shakes his head sadly, but says he will ask the Khwaja.

The men have started digging trenches. Hamoudi, the woman and the boy come up to Max.

Max looks at the boy and turns gently to the woman.

"The boy is as he is by the will of Allah," he says. "There is no medicine I can give you for the boy."

The woman sighs—I think a tear runs down her cheek. Then she says in a matter-of-fact voice:

"Then, Khwaja, will you give me some poison, for it is better he should not live?"

Max says gently that he cannot do that either.

She stares at him uncomprehendingly, then shakes her head angrily and goes away with the boy.

I wander up to the top of the mound where Macartney is busy with his survey. An Arab boy, full of importance, is staggering about with the pole. Mac, still unwilling to risk a word of Arabic, expresses his wishes by semaphoric gestures which do not always produce the desired result. Aristide, always obliging, comes to help.

I look all round me. To the north there is the line

of the Turkish hills, with a glittering spot which is
Mardin. West, south, and east there is only the
fertile steppe, which in spring will be green and starred
with flowers. Tells are dotted all over the landscape.
Here and there are Beduin tents in brown clusters.
Though there are villages on many of the Tells, you
cannot see them—in any case they are only a few
mud huts. Everything seems peaceful and remote from
man and the ways of civilization. I like Chagar Bazar,
and hope that he shall choose it. I would like to live
in a house built here. If we dig at Hamdun we shall
presumably live in Amuda. . . . Oh, no, I want *this*
Tell!

Evening comes. Max is pleased with the results. We
will come again tomorrow and continue the soundings.
This Tell, he believes, has been unoccupied since the
fifteenth century B.C., except for some intrusive Roman
and Islamic burials. There is excellent painted pottery
of the early Arpachiyah Tell Halaf type.

The Sheikh escorts us genially to the car.

"All that I have is yours, brother," he urges again.
"However poor it makes me!"

"How happy I shall be," says Max politely, "if it
falls to my lot to enrich you by digging here. Compensation will be paid as agreed with the French
authorities for any loss of crops, your men will be
paid good wages, land will be leased from you to
build a house, and, moreover, at the end of the season
a handsome present will be made to you personally."

"Ah," cries the Sheikh in high good humor, "I need
nothing! What is this talk of payment between
brothers?"

We depart on this altruistic note.

Two cold and wintry days spent at Tell Hamdun.
The results are reasonably good, but the fact that
part of the Tell is in Turkey is against it. The decision
seems clear for Chagar Bazar, with an additional con-
cession for Tell Brak, which could be combined with
the Chagar dig in a second season.

Now it only remains to get on with the arrangements for the spring. There is a suitable site to be chosen at Chagar for the house; there is the leasing of the house in Amuda for the time while the Chagar house is being built: there is the agreement to be drawn up with the Sheikh, and, most urgent, there is another money-order waiting at Hasetshe, which we must fetch without delay in case the wadis fill and the road is cut.

Hamoudi has been throwing money about rather grandly in Amuda lately, mindful of our "reputations." The spending of money seems a point of honor with Arabs—that is to say, the practice of entertaining notables in the coffee-house! To appear mean is a terrible dishonor. On the other hand, Hamoudi beats down remorselessly the charges of old women who bring milk and other old women who do our washing for what seems an incredibly small sum.

Max and I set off for Hasetshe in Mary, hoping for the best, though the sky is overcast and there is a faint drizzle of rain. We reach there without adventure, although the rain is now falling, and we wonder if we shall ever get back.

To our despair, when we get to the Post Office the Postmaster is out. No one knows where he is, but boys are dispatched in all directions to hunt for him.

The rain begins to fall in earnest. Max looks anxious, and says we shall never do it unless we can start back soon. We wait anxiously while the rain continues.

Suddenly the Postmaster appears, walking along in a leisurely fashion with a basket of eggs.

He greets us with pleasure and surprise. Max cuts short the usual politeness with an urgent plea for haste. We shall be cut off, he says.

"But why not?" says the Postmaster. "You will then have to remain here many days, which will be a pleasure to me personally. Hasetshe is a most agreeable town. Stay with us a long time," he urges hospitably.

Max renews his impassioned demand for haste. The Postmaster slowly unlocks drawers and searches in a desultory fashion, whilst still urging on us the desirability of making a long stay.

Curious, he says, that he cannot find this important envelope. He remembers it arriving, and he has said to himself: "One day the Khwaja will arrive for this." Therefore he has placed it in a place of safety, but where now can that place be? A clerk arrives to help, and the search is continued. Finally the letter is unearthed, and we go through the usual difficulty of obtaining cash. As before, this has to be collected from the Bazaar.

And still the rain falls! At last we have what we want. Max takes the precaution of buying bread and chocolate in case we spend a night or two *en route*, and we re-enter Mary and dash off at full speed. We negotiate the first wadi successfully, but at the second an ominous sight meets our eyes. The postal bus has stuck in it, and behind the postal bus is a line of cars waiting.

Everyone is down in the wadi—digging, fixing boards, yelling encouragement.

Max says despairingly: "We're here for the night."

It is a grim thought. I have spent many nights in the desert in cars, but never with enjoyment. One wakes cold and cramped, with pains all over.

However, this time we are lucky. The bus comes lumbering out with a roar, the other cars follow, and we come over at last. It is just in time—the water is rising rapidly.

Our journey back on the Amuda track is nightmarish in quality—one long continuous skid. Twice at least Mary turns completely around and faces determinedly in the direction of Hasetshe in spite of the chains on the wheels. This continuous skidding is a very peculiar feeling. Solid earth is not solid earth any longer. It has a fantastic nightmare quality.

We arrive after dark, and the household rushes out with cries of welcome, holding up lanterns.

I tumble out of Mary and slither my way to the door of our room. It is difficult to walk, because the mud has the peculiar quality of attaching itself to your feet in vast flat pancakes so heavy that you can hardly lift them.

Nobody, it appears, has expected to see us return, and the congratulations and El hamdu lillahs are vociferous.

The pancakes on my feet make me laugh. It is so exactly the sort of feeling you have in a dream.

Hamoudi laughs too, and says to Max: "It is good to have the Khatūn with us. All things make her laugh!"

Everything is now arranged. There has been a solemn meeting between Max, the Sheikh, and the French military officer of the Services Spéciaux in charge of the district. The rental of the land, the compensation, the obligations of each party—all is set down in black and white. The Sheikh alternates between saying that everything that he has is Max's and suggesting that about a thousand pounds in gold would be a fitting sum for him to receive!

He finally leaves, a much disappointed man, having evidently entertained the wildest dreams of affluence. He is consoled, however, by one clause of the contract, which provides that the house built for the Expedition shall, when the Expedition has finished with it, revert to him. His eyes brighten, and his vast red henna-dyed beard wags appreciatively.

"C'est tout de même un brave homme," says the French Capitaine when the Sheikh has finally departed. He shrugs his shoulders. "Il n'a pas le sou comme tout ces gens là!"

The negotiations for the renting of the Amuda house are complicated by the fact—which has only recently come to light—that instead of its being one house, as we imagined, it seems to be six! And as the six houses are inhabited by eleven families, the complications increase! The Armenian priest is merely the spokesman for all the varied householders!

An agreement is finally arrived at. On a definite date

the "houses" are to be vacant, and the interior treated
with two coats of whitewash!

So now all is settled. There is now the return journey to the coast to arrange. The cars will attempt to
reach Aleppo by way of Ras-el-Ain and Jerablus. It
is about two hundred miles, and there are many wadis
to cross in the early stages of the journey, but with
luck it may be done in two days. But with December
here the weather is bound to break soon. What will
the Khatūn do?

The Khatūn, ignobly, decides for a Wagon Lit. So
the taxi takes me to a strange little station, and presently a large and important blue sleeping-car comes
along behind a vast puffing engine. A conductor in
chocolate uniform leans out. Madame's baggage is
handed up, Madame herself is hoisted with difficulty
on to the high step from the permanent way.

"I think you're wise," says Max; "it's starting to
rain."

We both cry "See you in Alep!" The train starts! I
follow the conductor along the corridor. He flings open
the door of my compartment. The bed is made.

Here, once more, is civilization. *Le camping* is
ended. The conductor takes my passport, brings me a
bottle of mineral water, says: "We arrive at Alep at
six to-morrow morning. *Bonne nuit, Madame.*"

I might be going from Paris to the Riviera!

It seems strange, somehow, to find a Wagon Lit here
in the middle of nowhere. . . .

Alep!

Shops! A bath! My hair shampooed! Friends to see.

When Max and Mac roll in three days later, plastered with mud and carrying quantities of bustards
shot *en route,* I greet them with the superiority of one
inured once more to the fleshpots.

They have had plenty of adventures on the way—
the weather was bad, and I am satisfied that I chose
the better part.

The cook, it appears, demanded his chit as a driver

when paid off, and Max, before perjuring himself, ordered the cook to drive Mary once round the courtyard.

Jumping into the driving-seat, 'Isa started up, put the gear in reverse, and crashed heavily into the courtyard wall, knocking a large portion of it down. He was deeply injured when Max refused to guarantee him as a chauffeur! The testimonial as finally written announced that 'Isa had been our cook for three months, and had given us useful help with the car!

And so once more to Beyrout and a parting with Mac.

Egypt for us for the winter. Mac is to go to Palestine.

IV

FIRST SEASON AT
CHAGAR BAZAR

IT IS SPRING when we return to Beyrout. The first sight that greets us on the quay is Mac, but a Mac transformed.

He is smiling from ear to ear! No doubt about it—he is pleased to see us! Until now we have never known whether Mac has liked us or not. His feelings have been concealed behind his mask of polite impassiveness. But now it is clear that to him this is a reunion with friends. I cannot tell you how warming this is! From henceforth my nervousness with Mac vanishes. I even ask him whether every day since we last saw him he has sat on his plaid rug writing in his diary.

"Of course," says Mac, looking slightly surprised.

From Beyrout we proceed to Alep, and the usual business of getting in stores, etc., is accomplished. A chauffeur has been engaged for Mary—not this time an "economical" one picked up on the water-front, but a tall, worried-looking Armenian, who has at any rate a certain number of testimonials as to honesty and capacity. He has worked at one time for German engineers, and his principal disadvantage at first appearance is his voice, which is inclined to be a high and irritating whine. There is no doubt, however, that he will be an improvement on the sub-human Abdullah. Inquiries as to Aristide, whom we would have liked to have with us again, elicit the information that Aristide is now proudly in "Government service." He is driving a street watering-cart in Der-ez-zor!

The fateful date arrives, and we advance upon Amuda in two installments. Hamoudi and Mac, with Mary (now deprived of royal honors and known as Blue Mary, since she has received a somewhat lurid coat of blue paint), are to arrive first, and make sure that all is prepared for our reception. Max and I travel grandly by train to Kamichlie, there to spend the day transacting the necessary business with the French military authorities. It is about four o'clock when we leave Kamichlie for Amuda.

It is evident when we arrive that all has not gone according to plan. There is an air of confusion, loud recriminations, and plaints fill the air. Hamoudi has a distracted appearance and Mac a stoical one.

We soon learn the facts.

The house rented by us, which was to have been vacated, cleaned, whitewashed on a certain date now a week old, was found on the arrival of Hamoudi and Mac the day before to be innocent of whitewash, highly unclean, and still containing seven Armenian families!

What could be done in twenty-four hours has been done, but the result is not encouraging!

Hamoudi, by now well trained in the essential doctrine that the comfort of Khatūns comes first, has devoted all his energies to getting one room free of Armenians and live stock, and hastily whitewashing the walls. Two camp-beds have been set up in it for Max and myself. The rest of the house is still in chaos, and I gather that Hamoudi and Mac have spent an uncomfortable night.

But all will now be well, Hamoudi assures us, beaming with his usual irresistible smile.

The litigation and the recriminations that are now proceeding between the Armenian families and the Priest who was their spokesman are fortunately no concern of ours, and they are urged by Max to go and fight it out somewhere else!

Women, children, hens, cats, dogs—all weeping, wailing, screaming, shouting, abusing, praying, laughing, miauing, clucking and barking—depart slowly from the courtyard like some fantastic finale in an opera!

Everybody, we gather, has double-crossed everybody else! The financial chaos is complete, and the angry passions aroused between brothers, sisters, sisters-in-law, cousins, and great-grandparents are far too intricate for comprehension.

In the midst of chaos, however, our cook (a new cook, Dimitri by name) continues calmly to prepare an evening meal. We set to and eat with relish, and after that we retire to bed worn out.

To bed—but not to rest! I have never been one with an exaggerated distaste for mice. An odd mouse or so in a bedroom has left me unmoved, and I have even on one occasion had quite an affection for a persistent intruder named affectionately (though without any real knowledge as to sex) Elsie.

But our first night at Amuda is an experience I shall never forget.

No sooner have the lamps been extinguished than mice in their scores—I really believe in their hundreds—emerge from the holes in the walls and the floor. They run gaily over our beds, squeaking as they run. Mice across one's face, mice tweaking your hair—mice! mice! MICE! . . .

I switch on a torch. Horrible! The walls are covered with strange, pale, crawling cockroach-like creatures! A mouse is sitting on the foot of my bed attending to his whiskers!

Horrible crawling things are everywhere!

Max utters soothing words.

Just go to sleep, he says. Once you are asleep, none of these things will worry you.

Excellent advice, but not easy to act upon! One has first to get to sleep, and with mice taking healthy exercise and having their field sports all over you, that is hardly possible. Or it is not possible to me. Max seems able to do it all right!

I endeavor to subdue the shrinkings of the flesh. I do fall asleep for a short spell, but little feet running across my face wake me up. I flash on the light. The cockroaches have increased, and a large black spider is descending upon me from the ceiling!

So the night goes on, and I am ashamed to say that at two A.M. I become hysterical. When morning comes, I declare, I am going into Kamichlie to wait for the train, and I am going straight back to Alep! And from Alep I shall go straight back to England! I cannot stand this life! I will not stand it! I am going *home!*

In a masterly fashion Max deals with the situation. He rises, opens the door, calls to Hamoudi.

Five minutes later our beds have been dragged out into the courtyard. For a short while I lie gazing up at the peaceful starlit sky above. The air is cool and sweet. I fall asleep. Max, I rather fancy, breathes a sigh of relief before falling asleep himself.

You aren't really going back to Alep? Max inquires anxiously the next morning.

I blush a little over the remembrance of my hysterical outburst. No, I say; I wouldn't really go for the world. But I *am* going to continue to sleep in the courtyard!

Hamoudi explains soothingly that all will soon be well. The holes in the bedroom are being stopped up with plaster. More whitewash will be applied. Moreover, a cat is coming; it has been loaned out. It is a super-cat—a highly professional cat.

What sort of night, I ask Mac, did *he* have when he and Hamoudi arrived? Did things run over him all the time?

"I think so," said Mac, calm as always. "But I was asleep."

Wonderful Mac!

Our cat arrives at dinner-time. I shall never forget that cat! It is, as Hamoudi has announced, a highly professional cat. It knows the job for which it has been engaged, and proceeds to get on with it in a truly specialized manner.

Whilst we dine, it crouches in ambush behind a packing-case. When we talk, or move, or make too much noise, it gives us an impatient look.

"I must request of you," the look says, "to be *quiet*. How can I get on with the job without co-operation?"

So fierce is the cat's expression that we obey at once, speak in whispers, and eat with as little clinking of plates and glasses as possible.

Five times during the meal a mouse emerges and runs across the floor, and five times our cat springs. The sequel is immediate. There is no Western dallying, no playing with the victim. The cat simply bites off the mouse's head, crunches it up, and proceeds to the rest of the body! It is rather horrible and completely businesslike.

The cat stays with us five days. After those five days no mice appear. The cat then leaves us, and the mice never come back. I have never known before or since such a professional cat. It had no interest in us, it never demanded milk or a share of our food. It was cold, scientific, and impersonal. A very accomplished cat!

Now we are settled in. The walls have been whitewashed, the window-sills and door painted, a carpenter and his four sons have established themselves in the courtyard, and are making our furniture to order.

"Tables," says Max, "above all, *tables!* One cannot have too many tables."

I put in a plea for a chest of drawers, and Max kindly allows me a wardrobe with pegs.

Then the carpenters return to making more tables— tables on which to spread our pottery, a drawing-table for Mac, a table off which to dine, a table for my typewriter. . . .

Mac draws out a towel-horse and the carpenters start upon it. The old man brings it proudly to my room on completion. It looks different from Mac's drawing, and when the carpenter sets it down I see why. It has colossal feet, great curved scrolls of feet. They stick out so that, wherever you put it, you invariably trip over them.

Ask him, I say to Max, why he has made these feet instead of sticking to the design he was given?

The old man looks at us with dignity.

"I made them this way," he says, "so that they should be beautiful. I wanted this that I have made to be a thing of beauty!"

To this cry of the artist there could be no response. I bow my head, and resign myself to tripping up over those hideous feet for the rest of the season!

Outside, in the far corner of the courtyard, some masons are making me a mud-brick lavatory.

I ask Mac that evening at dinner what his first architectural job has been.

"This is my first bit of *practical* work," he replies— "your lavatory!"

He sighs gloomily, and I feel very sympathetic. It will not, I fear, look well in Mac's memoirs when he comes to write them.

The budding dreams of a young architect should not find their first expression in a mud-brick lavatory for his patron's wife!

To-day the Capitaine Le Boiteux and two French nuns come to tea. We greet them in the village and bring them back to the house. Set proudly before the front door is the carpenter's latest achievement—my lavatory seat!

The house is now organized The room where we first slept, and which is still cockroach-ridden at night, is the drawing-office. Here Mac can work in solitude, free from human contacts. He is, in any case, quite unmoved by cockroaches!

Next to it is the dining-room. Farther along is the antika-room, where our finds will be stored, where pottery will be mended, and objects sorted and classified and labelled. (It is full of tables!) Then there is a small office-cum-sitting-room, where my typewriter reposes, and where the deck-chairs are set up. In what was the Priest's house are three bedrooms—free from mice (thanks to our cat), free from cockroaches (thanks to the plentiful whitewash?), unfortunately *not* free from fleas!

We are to suffer a good deal from fleas. The flea has abundant vitality, and seems to have a miraculously protected life. It thrives on Keatings and Flit, and every kind of flea-killer. Anointing beds with carbolic merely stimulates fleas to even greater displays of athletics. It is not, I explain to Mac, so much the bites of fleas. It is their tireless energy, their never-ending hopping races round and round one's middle that wears one out. Impossible to drop off to sleep when fleas are holding the nightly sports round and round the waist.

Max suffers from fleas worse than I do. One day I find and kill one hundred and seven in the band of his pyjamas! He finds fleas, he says, enervating. It would appear that I only get the overflow of fleas—the ones, that is, which have not been able to take up their abode on Max. Mine are second-class, inferior fleas, ineligible for the high jumps!

Mac, it seems, has *no* fleas. This seems very unfair. They apparently do not fancy him as a sports ground!

Life now settles down on its accustomed round. Max departs at dawn every morning to the mound.

Most days I go with him, though occasionally I stay
at home to deal with other things—*e.g.* mending of
the pottery and objects, labelling, and sometimes to ply
my own trade on the typewriter. Mac also stays at
home two days a week, busy in the drawing-office.

It is a long day on the mound if I go, but not too
long if the weather is good. It is cold until the sun is
well up, but later it is very lovely. Flowers are springing up everywhere, mostly the little red anemones,
as I incorrectly call them (ranunculus is, I believe, the
real term).

A nucleus of workers have been brought by Max
from Jerablus, Hamoudi's home town. Hamoudi's two
sons, after finishing working at Ur for the season, have
come to us. Yahya, the elder, is tall, with a wide,
cheerful grin. He is like a friendly dog. Alawi, the
younger, is good looking, and probably the more intelligent of the two. But he has a quick temper, and
quarrels sometimes flare up. An elderly cousin, Abd es
Salaam, is also a foreman. Hamoudi, after starting
us off, is to return home.

Once the work has been started on by the strangers
from Jerablus, workmen from the spot hasten to be
enrolled. The men of the Sheikh's village have already
begun work. Now men from neighboring villages begin
to arrive by ones and twos. There are Kurds, men from
over the Turkish border, some Armenians, and a few
Yezidis (so-called devil-worshippers)—gentle, melancholy looking men, prone to be victimized by the others.

The system is a simple one. The men are organized
into gangs. Men with any previous experience of digging, and men who seem intelligent and quick to learn,
are chosen as pickmen. Men, boys, and children are
paid the same wage. Over and above that there is
(dear to the Eastern heart) bakshish. That is to say,
a small cash payment on each object found.

The pickman of each gang has the best chance of
finding objects. When his square of ground has been
traced out to him, he starts upon it with a pick. After
him comes the spademan. With his spade he shovels the

earth into baskets, which three or four "basket-boys"
then carry away to a spot appointed as dump. As they
turn the earth out, they sort through it for any likely
object missed by the Qasmagi and the spademan, and
since they are often little boys with sharp eyes, not
infrequently some small amulet or bead gives them a
good reward. Their finds they tie up in a corner of
their ragged drapperies to be produced at the end of
the day. Occasionally they appeal to Max with an
object, and upon his reply, ". . . keep it, or Shiluh,
remove it," its fate is decided. This applies to small
objects—amulets, fragments of pottery, beads, etc.
When a group of pots in position, or the bones of a
burial, or traces of mud-brick walls are found, then
the foreman in charge calls for Max, and things proceed with due care. Max or Mac scrape carefully
round the group of pots—or the dagger, or whatever
the find is—with a knife, clearing the earth away, blowing away loose dust. Then the find is photographed
before being removed, and roughly drawn in a notebook.

The tracing out of buildings when they appear is
also a delicate business needing the specialist. The
foreman usually takes the pick himself and follows the
mud-brick carefully, but an intelligent, though hitherto
inexperienced pickman, soon picks up the art of tracing
mud-brick, and before long you will hear him say
confidently during his digging: "Hadha libn" (This is
mud-brick).

Our Armenian workmen are, on the whole, the
most intelligent. Their disadvantage is their provocative
attitude—they always manage to inflame the tempers
of the Kurds and Arabs. Quarrelling is, in any case,
almost continuous. All our workmen have hot tempers,
and all carry with them the means of expressing themselves—large knives, bludgeons, and a kind of mace or
knobkerry! Heads are cut open, and furious figures
are entangled with each other in fierce struggles and
torn asunder, whilst Max loudly proclaims the rules
of the dig. For all who fight there will be a fine!

"Settle your quarrels in the hours outside the work. On the work there is to be no fighting. On the work I am your father, and what your father says must be done! Nor will I listen to causes of the dispute, or otherwise I should do nothing else! It takes two to fight and all who fight will be fined equally."

The men listen, nod their heads. "It is true. He is our father! There must be no fighting, or something of value and good price might be destroyed."

Fights, however, still break out. For persistent fighting a man is sacked.

This, I may say, doesn't mean permanent dismissal. A man is sometimes sacked for one day, two days; and, even when dismissed altogether, usually reappears after next pay day with a demand to be taken on for the next shift.

Pay-day is fixed, after some experiment, after a period of about ten days. Some of the men come from fairly distant villages, bringing their food with them. This (a sack of flour and a few onions) is usually exhausted in ten days, and the man then asks to go home, since his food is ended. One of the great disadvantages, we find, is that the men do not work regularly. As soon as they are paid they quit work. "I have money now. Why should I continue to work? I will go home." In about a fortnight, the money spent, the man returns and asks to be taken on again. It is annoying from our point of view, as a gang that has got used to working together is far more efficient than a new combination.

The French have their own way of dealing with this habit, which caused them great difficulty when work was in progress on the railway. They used to keep their workmen permanently half-pay in arrear. This ensured their working continuously. The Lieutenant advised Max to adopt this system, but on consultation we decided not to do so, since from Max's point of view it seemed basically unfair. The men had earned their money and were entitled to be paid in full. So we had to put up with the continuous going and coming. It

makes a lot more work with the pay-book, which has
continually to be revised and altered.

Having arrived on the mound at half-past six, a halt
is called for breakfast at eight-thirty. We eat hard-
boiled eggs and flaps of Arab bread, and Michel (the
chauffeur) produces hot tea, which we drink from
enamel mugs, sitting on the top of the mound, the sun
just pleasantly warm, and the morning shadows making
the landscape incredibly lovely, with the blue Turkish
hills to the north, and all around tiny springing flowers
of scarlet and yellow. The air is wonderfully sweet. It
is one of those moments when it is good to be alive.
The foremen are grinning happily; small children driving cows come and gaze at us shyly. They are dressed
in incredible rags, their teeth gleam white as they smile.
I think to myself how happy they look, and what a
pleasant life it is; like the fairy stories of old, wandering about over the hills herding cattle, sometimes sitting
and singing.

At this time of day, the so-called fortunate children
in European lands are setting out for the crowded class-
room, going in out of the soft air, sitting on benches or
at desks, toiling over letters of the alphabet, listening to
a teacher, writing with cramped fingers. I wonder to
myself whether, one day a hundred years or so ahead,
we shall say in shocked accents: "In *those* days they
actually made poor little children go to *school,* sitting
inside buildings at desks for *hours a day!* Isn't it terrible
to think of! Little *children!*"

Bringing myself back from this vision of the future,
I smile at a little girl with a tattooed forehead, and
offer her a hard-boiled egg.

She immediately shakes her head in alarm and hurriedly moves on. I feel I have committed a solecism.

The foremen blow their whistles. Back to work. I
wander slowly round the mound, pausing from time
to time at various parts of the work. One is always
hoping to be on the spot just when an interesting find
turns up. Of course, one never is! After leaning hopefully on my shooting-stick for twenty minutes watching

Mohammed Hassan and his gang, I move on to 'Isa Daoud, to learn later that the find of the day—a lovely pot of incised ware—was found just after I had moved my pitch.

I have another job, too. I keep an observant eye on the basket-boys, for some of the lazier of these, when taking their baskets to the dump, do not return at once. They sit down in the sun to sort through the earth from their basket, and often spend a comfortable quarter of an hour this way! Even more reprehensible, some of them curl up comfortably on the dump and enjoy a good sleep!

Towards the end of the week, in my rôle of master spy, I report my findings.

"That very little basket-boy, the one with the yellow head-dress, is first-class; he never slacks for a minute. I should sack Salah Hassan; he's always asleep on the dump. Abdul Aziz is a bit of a slacker, and so is the one in that ragged blue coat."

Max agrees that Salah Hassan is for it, but says that Abdul Aziz has such sharp eyes that he never misses anything.

Every now and then during the morning, as Max comes round, a spurt of entirely fictitious energy is shown. Everyone shouts "Yallah!" yells, sings, dances. The basket-boys rush panting to and from the dump, tossing their empty baskets in the air and yelling. Then it all dies down again, and things go even more slowly than before.

The foremen keep up a series of encouraging cries of "Yallah!" and a kind of formula of sarcasm, which has presumably become quite meaningless by constant repetition.

"Are you old women, the way you move? Surely you are not men? What slowness! Like broken-down cows!" etc., etc.

I wander away from the work and around the far side of the mound. Here, looking north towards the blue line of hills, I sit down among the flowers and go into a pleasing coma.

A party of women are coming from the distance towards me. By the gaiety of their coloring they are Kurdish women. They are busy digging up roots and picking leaves.

They make a bee-line for me. Presently they are sitting round me in a circle.

Kurdish women are gay and handsome. They wear bright colors. These women have turbans of bright orange round their heads, their clothes are green and purple and yellow. Their heads are carried erect on their shoulders, they are tall, with a backward stance, so that they always look proud. They have bronze faces, with regular features, red cheeks, and usually blue eyes.

The Kurdish men nearly all bear a marked resemblance to a colored picture of Lord Kitchener that used to hang in my nursery as a child. The brick-red face, the big brown moustache, the blue eyes, the fierce and martial appearance!

In this part of the world Kurdish and Arab villages are about equal in number. They lead the same lives and belong to the same religion, but not for a moment could you mistake a Kurdish woman for an Arab woman. Arab women are invariably modest and retiring; they turn their face away when you speak to them; if they look at you, they do so from a distance. If they smile, it is shyly, and with a half-averted face. They wear mostly black or dark colors. And no Arab woman would ever come up and speak to a man! A Kurdish woman has no doubt that she is as good as a man or better! They come out of their houses and make jokes to any man, passing the time of day with the utmost amiability. They make no bones about bullying their husbands. Our Jerablus workmen, unused to Kurds, are profoundly shocked.

"Never," exclaims one, "did I think to hear a respectable woman address her husband in such a way! Truly, I did not know which way to look."

My Kurdish women this morning are examining me with frank interest and exchanging ribald comments with each other. They are very friendly, nod at me, and laugh, ask questions, then sigh and shake their heads as they tap their lips.

They are clearly saying: "What a pity we cannot understand each other!" They take up a fold of my skirt and examine it with interest; they pinch my sleeve. They point up at the mound. I am the Khwaja's woman? I nod. They fire off more questions, then laugh at the realization that they cannot get answers. No doubt they want to know all about my children and my miscarriages!

They try to explain to me what they do with the herbs and plants they are picking. Ah, but it is no good!

Another great burst of laughter breaks out. They get up, smile, and nod and drift off, talking and laughing. They are like great gay-colored flowers. . . .

They live in hovels of mud, with perhaps a few cooking-pots as all their possessions, yet their gaiety and laughter are unforced. They find life good, with a Rabelaisian flavor. They are handsome, and full-blooded and gay.

My little Arab girl passes, driving the cows. She smiles at me shyly, then quickly averts her eyes.

In the distance I hear the foreman's whistle. Fidos! It is twelve-thirty—an hour's break for lunch.

I retrace my steps to where Max and Mac are waiting. Michel is setting out the lunch that Dimitri has packed. We have slices of cold mutton, more hard-boiled egg, flaps of Arab bread, and cheese—the local cheese of the country for Max and Mac; goat's cheese, strong flavored, a pale-grey in color, and slightly hairy. I have the sophisticated variety of synthetic *gruyère*, silver-papered in its round cardboard box. Max looks at it contemptuously. After the food, there are oranges and enamel mugs of hot tea.

After lunch we go to look at the site of our house.

It is some hundred yards beyond the village and the Sheikh's house, to the south-east of the mound. It is all traced out, and I ask Mac doubtfully if the rooms aren't very small. He looks amused, and explains that

that is the effect of the open space surrounding it. The house is to be built with a central dome; it will have a big living-and-working-room in the middle, with two rooms off that on each side. The kitchen quarters will be separate. On to the main structure we can add additional rooms if the dig is prolonged and we need them.

A little way from the house we are going to prospect for a new well, so as not to depend on the Sheikh's well. Max selects the spot and then goes back to the work.

I stay for a while, and watch Mac getting things done by means of gestures, head shakings, whistles—everything except the spoken word!

At about four o'clock Max starts going round the gangs and bakshishing the men. As he comes to each one, they stop, line up roughly, and produce the small finds of the day. One of the more enterprising of the basket-boys has cleaned his acquisitions with spit!

Opening his immense book, Max starts operations.

"Qasmagi?" (Pickman.)

"Hassan Mohammed."

What has Hassan Mohammed got? Half a large broken pot, many fragments of pottery, a bone knife, a scrap or two of copper.

Max turns the collection over, flings away ruthlessly what is rubbish—usually those things which have inflamed the pickman's highest hopes—puts bone implements in one of the small boxes that Michel carries, beads in another. Fragments of pottery go in one of the big baskets that a small boy carries.

Max announces the price: twopence ha'penny, or possibly fourpence, and writes it down in the book. Hassan Mohammed repeats the sum, storing it away in his capacious memory.

Terrific arithmetic lies ahead at the end of the week. When each daily sum has been added up and joined to the daily rate of pay the amount is then paid over. The man paid usually knows exactly what he is to receive!

Sometimes he will say: "It is not enough—there should be twopence more." Or just as often: "You have given me too much; fourpence less is what is owing me." They are seldom wrong. Occasional errors arise owing to the similarity of names. There are often three or four Daoud Mohammeds, and they have to be further distinguished by Daoud Mohammed Ibraham, or Daoud Mohammed Suliman.

Max goes on to the next man.

"Your name?"

"Ahmad Mohammed."

Ahmad Mohammed has not very much. Strictly speaking he has nothing at all that we want; but encouragement must be given, however small, so Max selects a few sherds of pottery and throws them into the basket and announces a couple of farthings.

Next come the basket-boys. Ibrahim Daoud has an exciting-looking object, which is only, alas, a fragment of an incised Arab pipe-stem! But now comes little Abdul Jehar, proffering doubtfully some tiny beads, and another object that Max snatches at with approval. A cylinder seal, intact, and of a good period—a really good find. Little Abdul is commended, and five francs is written down to his name. A murmur of excitement breaks out.

There is no doubt that to the workmen, gamblers all by nature, the uncertainty of the business is its principal attraction. And it is astonishing how a run of luck will attend certain gangs. Sometimes when new ground is being broken Max will say: "I shall put Ibrahim and his gang on this outer wall; they've found far too much lately. Now poor old Rainy George has had no luck lately. I'll put him on to a good place."

But lo and behold! In Ibrahim's patch, the houses of the poorest quarter of the old city, straightaway is found a *cache* of an earthenware pot containing a heap of gold earrings—the dowry, perhaps, of a daughter of olden days, and up goes Ibrahim's bakshish; and Rainy George, digging in a promising cemetery area where finds should abound, gets unaccountably sparse burials.

The men who have been bakshished go back to work in desultory fashion. Max goes on till he comes to the last gang.

It is now half an hour before sunset. The whistle blows. Everybody yells "Fidos! Fidos!" They fling baskets in the air, catch them, and run headlong down the hill, yelling and laughing.

Another day's work is over. Those who come from villages two or three miles away start to walk home. Our finds, in their baskets and boxes, are brought down the hill and packed carefully into Mary. A few men whose homes are on our route clamber on to Mary's roof. We set off home. Another day is over.

By a curious coincidence, our well that we have started to dig proves to be at the exact spot where a well has been dug in antiquity. This creates such an effect that a few days later five grave bearded gentlemen wait upon Max as he descends from the mound.

They have come, they explain, from their villages many miles distant. They are in need of more water. The Khwaja knows the places where the wells are hidden—those wells that the Romans had. If he will indicate the places to them they will be eternally grateful.

Max explains that it is pure chance that we have hit upon the spot where a well formerly existed.

The grave gentlemen smile politely but disbelievingly.

"'You have great wisdom, Khwaja; that is known. The secrets of antiquity are to you an open book. Where cities were, where wells were, all these things you know. Therefore, indicate to us the right places to dig and there shall be gifts."

None of Max's protestations are believed. Rather is he regarded as a magician who keeps his secrets. He knows, they murmur, but he will not say.

"I wish to goodness we'd never struck on that beastly Roman well," says Max gloomily. "It's causing me no end of trouble."

Complications arise when the men have to be paid. The official currency of the country is the French franc. But in this part of the world the Turkish mejidi has been in use so long that the conservative inhabitants regard nothing else as satisfactory. The bazaars deal in that currency though the banks do not. Our men refuse persistently to be paid in anything except the mejidi.

Consequently, having got the official currency from the bank, Michel has then to be dispatched to the bazaars to change it into the illegal currency that is the *"effectif"* locally.

The mejidi is a large, heavy coin. Michel staggers in with trays of these—handfuls, bagfuls! He pours them out upon the table. They are all very dirty, and smell of garlic!

We have nightmare evenings before pay-day counting out mejidis, almost asphyxiated with the smell of them!

Michel is invaluable in many ways. He is honest, punctual, and most scrupulous. Unable to read or write, he can carry the most complicated accounts in his head, returning from market with a long string of purchases, sometimes as many as thirty, reciting the price of each accurately, and putting down the exact amount of change. He never makes a single mistake in accountancy.

He is, on the other hand, overbearing in the extreme, extremely quarrelsome with all Mohammedans, very obstinate, and with an unfortunately heavy hand on machinery. *Forca!* he says, his eyes gleaming, and immediately afterwards an ominous snap is heard.

Even more disastrous are his economies. Putrescent bananas and dried-up oranges he is chagrined to find unappreciated. "Were there, then, no good ones?" "Yes, but more expensive. These are more economical."

It is a great word—*Economia!* It costs us a good deal in pure waste.

Michel's third slogan is *"Sawi proba"* (Make trial).

He says it in all kinds of tone of voice—hopefully, coaxingly, eagerly, confidently, sometimes despairingly. The result is usually unfortunate.

Our washerwoman having been unaccountably slow in delivering my cotton frocks, I venture to put on the Empire Builder's wife's shantung coat and skirt, which I have previously not had the courage to wear.

Max takes one look at me.

"What on earth have you got on?"

I say defensively that it is nice and cool.

"You can't wear that," says Max. "Go and take it off."

"I must wear it. I've bought it."

"It's too frightful. You look like the most offensive kind of *memsahib*—straight from Poonah!"

I admit sadly that I have had a suspicion to that effect.

Max says encouragingly: "Put on the greenish buff with the Tell Halaf running lozenge pattern."

"I wish," I say crossly, "that you would not use pottery terms for describing my clothes. It's lime-green! And a running lozenge is a disgusting term—like something half-sucked and left by a child on a village shop counter. How you can think up such disgusting descriptions for pottery patterns I cannot think!"

What an imagination you have, says Max. And the running lozenge is an extremely attractive Tell Halaf pattern.

He draws it for me on a piece of paper, and I say that I know all about it, and that it is a most attractive pattern. It's the description that's so revolting.

Max looks at me sadly and shakes his head.

As we pass through the village of Hanzir we hear the following conversation.

"Who are these?"

"They are the foreigners who dig."

Gravely an old gentleman surveys us.

"How beautiful they are," he sighs. "They are full of money!"

An old woman rushes up to Max.

"Khwaja! Mercy; intercede for my son. They have taken him away to Damascus—to prison. He is a good man, he has done nothing—nothing at all, I swear it!"

"Why, then, did they take him to prison?"

"For nothing. It is an injustice. Save him for me."

"But what has he done, mother?"

"Nothing. I swear it before God. Before God, it is true! He had done nothing but kill a man!"

Now a new anxiety arises. Several of the men from Jerablus fall ill. They are in tents at Chagar Bazar. Three men are laid up, and difficulty arises because the other men will not go near them. They will not take them food or water.

This avoidance of the sick is very strange. But, then, everything seems strange in a community where the value of human life is not accounted as important.

"They will starve if no food is taken to them," says Max.

Their fellow-workmen shrug their shoulders.

"Inshallah, if it is God's will."

The foremen, albeit reluctantly, vindicate their acquaintance with civilization and render some grudging service. Max broaches delicately the question of hospital. He can arrange with the French authorities for the two men who are seriously ill to be admitted to hospital.

Yahya and Alawi shake their heads doubtfully. It will be a disgrace to go to hospital, for in hospital disgraceful things happen. Death is always preferable to disgrace.

I think wildly of mistaken diagnoses, of neglect. "What are these disgraceful things that have occurred?" I asked.

Max goes deeper into the subject. Then, after a

long series of questions and answers which I do not follow, he turns and explains.

A man was admitted to hospital and there he was given an enema—

"Yes," I say, waiting for the story to proceed.

Max says that that is all.

"But did the man die?"

"No, but he would have preferred to die."

"What?" I cry incredulously.

Max says that it is so. The man returned to his village, nursing a deep and bitter grievance. Such an indignity was too deep! Death would to him have been preferable.

Accustomed as we are to our Western ideas of the importance of life, it is difficult to adjust one's thoughts to a different scale of values. And yet to the Oriental mind it is simple enough. Death is bound to come— it is as inevitable as birth, whether it comes early or late is entirely at the will of Allah. And that belief, that acquiescence, does away with what has become the curse of our present-day world—anxiety. There may not be freedom from want, but there is certainly freedom from fear. And idleness is a blessed and natural state—work is the unnatural necessity.

I think of an old beggar we came across in Persia. He had a white beard and a dignified and noble mien. He spoke proudly, for all his outstretched hand.

"Give me of your munificence a trifle, oh Prince. It concerns me that I may avoid death."

The problem of the two ill men becomes more acute. Max goes into Kamichlie and lays his troubles before the French Commandant. The officers there are always kind and helpful. Max is introduced to the French military doctor, and the latter drives out with him to the mound and examines the patients.

He confirms our fears that the men are really ill. One man, he says, must have been already in a very serious

state of health when he came to us, and there could
never have been much hope of his recovery. He recommends that they should both be brought into hospital.
The men are persuaded to agree, and they are driven
there forthwith.

The French doctor also very kindly gives us some
really powerful aperient medicine, which will, he assures us, move a horse!

This is certainly needed, for the men are constantly
coming to Max with graphic accounts of constipation,
and ordinary laxatives seem to have no effect whatever.

One of our sick men has died in hospital. The other
is well on the way to recovery. Word comes to us of
the death two days after it has occurred, and we learn
that the man is already buried.

Alawi comes to us with a grave face.

It is a question, he says, of our reputation. . . .

My heart sinks slightly. The word reputation always
precedes the expenditure of money.

This man, he goes on, has died far from his home.
He has been buried here. That, in Jerablus, will be a
great reflection upon us.

But we cannot help the man's dying, says Max. He
was already an ill man when he came, and we have
done all we can.

Alawi waves death aside. Death is nothing. It is not
the man's *death* that matters. It is the *burial*.

For what will be the position of this man's relations—of his family? He has been buried in a strange
place. Then they will have to leave home and come
to where his grave is. It is a disgrace for a man not to
return to be buried in his home town.

Max says that he doesn't see what he can do about
it now. The man *is* buried. What does Alawi suggest—
a present of money to the sorrowing family?

That will be acceptable, yes. But what Alawi is really
suggesting is disinterment.

"What! Dig him up again?"

"Yes, Khwaja. Send the body back to Jerablus. Then all will be done honorably, and your reputation will not suffer."

Max says that he does not know whether such a thing can be managed. It doesn't seem to him practicable.

Finally we go into Kamichlie and have a consultation with the French authorities. They obviously consider that we are mad!

Unexpectedly, this stiffens Max's determination. It is, he agrees, doubtless foolish, but is it *possible?*

The doctor shrugs his shoulders. But yes, it is *possible!* There will be forms—a lot of forms. *"Et des timbres, beaucoup de timbres."* "Naturally," says Max, "that is inevitable!"

Things are set under way. A taxi-driver, shortly making the return journey to Jerablus, enthusiastically accepts the task of conveying the (suitably disinfected) dead body. A workman, cousin of the dead man, will go in charge. All is arranged.

First, disinterment; then the signing of many forms and the attaching of stamps; the attendance of the military doctor armed with a large formalin spray; the bestowing of the body in the coffin; more formalin; the coffin is sealed up, the taxi-driver hoists it cheerfully into position.

"Hola!" he cries. "We shall have a gay journey! We must be careful our brother does not fall off on the way!"

The whole proceedings are now taking on that intense jocularity that can only be paralleled by the spirit of an Irish wake. The taxi drives off, with the driver and the cousin singing songs at the top of their voices. This, you feel, is a wonderful occasion for both of them! They are thoroughly enjoying themselves.

Max breathes a sigh of relief. He has affixed the last stamp and paid the final fees. The necessary forms (a voluminous sheaf) have been entrusted to the taxi-driver.

"Ah, well," says Max, "that is the end of *that!*"

He is wrong. The journey of the dead man, Abdullah Hamid, could be made into a poetical saga. There seems a moment when his body shall never know repose.

The body duly arrives at Jerablus. It is received with the proper lamentations, and with, we gather, a certain pride, so splendid has been its journey. There is a big celebration—a feast, in fact. The taxi-man, calling upon Allah, proceeds on his journey to Alep. It is realized, after he has gone, that the all-important "forms" have gone with him.

Chaos ensues. Without the necessary form the dead man cannot be buried. Is it necessary then, that he shall be returned to Kamichlie? Hot disputes arise on these points. Messages are dispatched—to the French authorities at Kamichlie, to us, to the very problematical address of the taxi-driver in Alep. Everything is done in a leisurely Arab fashion—and in the meantime Abdullah Hamid remains unburied.

How long, I ask Max anxiously, does the effect of formalin last? A fresh set of forms (complete with *les timbres*) are obtained and sent to Jerablus. Word comes that the corpse is about to be sent back by rail to Kamichlie. Urgent wires fly to and fro.

Suddenly all ends well. The taxi-man reappears in Jerablus, flourishing the forms.

"What an oversight!" he exclaims. The funeral proceeds in order and decency. Our reputation, Alawi assures us, is safe! The French authorities still consider we are mad. Our workmen gravely approve. Michel is outraged—what absence of *economia!* To relieve his feelings he hammers *tutti* loudly under the windows in the early hours of the morning until told forcefully to stop.

Tutti is the general name for all construction and usages of petrol tins. What Syria would do without the petrol tin one cannot imagine! Women fetch water from the well in petrol tins. Petrol tins are cut and hammered in strips on roofs and to mend houses.

It is Michel's ambition, he tells us in a burst of confidence, to have a house completely made of *tutti*.

"It will be beautiful," he says wistfully, "very beautiful."

V

FIN DE SAISON

CHAGAR BAZAR IS turning out well, and B. comes out from London as additional help for the last month.

It is interesting to watch B. and Mac together—they are such a complete contrast. B. is definitely a social animal, Mac an unsocial one. They get on very well together, but look at each other in puzzled wonderment.

On a day when we are going into Kamichlie, B. suddenly expresses concern.

"Seems rather bad luck leaving old Mac alone all day? Perhaps I'd better stay with him."

"Mac likes being alone," I assure him.

B. looks incredulous. He goes off to the drawing-office.

"Look here, Mac, like me to stay behind? Rather boring being alone all day."

A look of consternation crosses Mac's face.

"Oh," he says, "I've been looking forward to it."

"Queer chap he is," says B. as we bounce from rut to rut on the way to Kamichlie. "You know that

106

sunset last night? Beautiful! I was up on the roof
looking at it. Found Mac there. I was a bit enthusiastic,
I admit, but old Mac, he didn't say a word. Didn't
even *answer*. Yet I suppose he went up there to look
at it?"

"Yes, he usually goes up there in the evenings."

"It seems so odd he doesn't *say* anything, then."

I picture Mac on the roof, aloof and silent, B. buzz-
ing enthusiastically beside him.

Later, no doubt, Mac in his scrupulously neat room
will sit upon the plaid rug and write in his diary. . . .

"I mean, you'd think, wouldn't you . . ." B. goes
on perseveringly, but is interrupted as Michel, swerv-
ing across the road with diabolical intentions, steps
heavily on the accelerator and charges a party of Arabs
—two old women and a man with a donkey.

They scatter, screaming, and Max surpasses himself
in swearing angrily at Michel. What the hell does he
think he's doing? He might have killed them!

That apparently, was more or less Michel's intention.

"What would it have mattered?" he asks, flinging
both hands in the air and allowing the car to take its
own course. "They are Mohammedans, are they not?"

After enunciating this, according to his views, highly
Christian sentiment, he relapses into the martyred
silence of one misunderstood. What kind of Christians
are these, he seems to be saying to himself, weak and
irresolute in the faith!

Max lays it down as a positive rule that no attempted murder of Mohammedans is to be permitted.

Michel murmurs sadly under his breath:

"It would be better if *all* Mohammedans were dead!"

Apart from our usual business in Kamichlie of visits
to the Bank, shopping at M. Yannakos', and a polite
call on the French, B. has business of his own—
namely, to collect a parcel sent after him from England
and consisting of two pairs of pajamas.

An official notification has been received by us that

the parcel in question is waiting at the Post Office, and so to the Post Office we go.

The Postmaster is not in evidence, but is summoned to the post of duty by a wall-eyed underling. He arrives yawning, heavily dressed in lurid striped pajamas. Although obviously aroused from heavy slumber, he is polite and amiable, shakes hands all round, inquires as to the progress of our excavations: Have we found any gold? Will we drink a cup of coffee with him? And thus courtesy having been satisfied, we drift to the subject of mail. Our letters now come to the Post Office at Amuda——not a very happy plan, as the elderly Postmaster in Amuda regards them as so precious and valuable that he frequently locks them away in the safe deposit for valuables and forgets to hand them out.

B.'s parcel, however, has been detained in Kamichlie, and we now start negotiations for its delivery.

"Yes, certainly there is such a parcel," says the Postmaster. "It has come from London England. Ah, what a great city that must be! How much I would like to see it! It is addressed to a Monsieur B." Ah, this is Monsieur B., our new colleague? He shakes hands with B. again and utters some polite compliments. B. replies socially and politely in Arabic.

After this interlude we return to the question of the parcel. Yes, says the Postmaster, it has been here —actually here in the office! But it is here no longer. It has been removed to the custody of the Customs. Monsieur B. must realize that parcels are subject to Custom dues.

B. says that it is personal wearing apparel.

The Postmaster says: "No doubt, no doubt; but that is the affair of the Customs."

"We must, then, go to the Customs office?"

"That will be the proper procedure," agrees the Postmaster. "Not that it will be any use going today. Today is Wednesday, and on Wednesdays the Customs are closed."

"Tomorrow, then?"

"Yes, tomorrow the Customs will be open."

"Sorry," says B. to Max. "I suppose it means I shall have to come in again tomorrow to get my parcel."

The Postmaster says that certainly Monsieur B. will have to come in tomorrow, but that even tomorrow he will not be able to get his parcel.

"Why not?" demands B.

"Because, after the formalities of the Customs have been settled, the parcel must then go through the Post Office."

"You mean, I shall have to come on here?"

"Precisely. And that will not be possible tomorrow, for tomorrow the Post Office will be closed," says the Postmaster triumphantly.

We go into the subject in detail, but officialdom triumphs at every turn. On no day of the week, apparently, are both the Customs and the Post Office open!

We immediately turn and upbraid poor B., and ask him why on earth he can't bring his beastly pajamas with him instead of having them sent on by post!

"Because," says B., defending himself, "they are very special pajamas."

"They should be," says Max, "considering all the trouble they are going to cause! This lorry goes to and from the dig every day; not into Kamichlie as a postal service!"

We try to persuade the Postmaster to let B. sign the P.O. forms now, but he is adamant. P.O. formalities are always undertaken *after* the Customs. Defeated, we go sadly out of the Post Office, and the Postmaster, presumably, returns to bed.

Michel comes up excitedly and says he has made a most advantageous bargain in oranges. He has bought two hundred oranges at a most economical price. As usual, he is sworn at. How does he think we are going to get through two hundred oranges before they go bad—that is to say, if they are not bad already?

Some of them, Michel admits, are perhaps a trifle on the stale side, but they are very cheap, and there is a great reduction for taking the two hundred. Max agrees to inspect them, and on doing so immediately turns them down. Most of them are already covered with green mould!

Michel murmurs sadly: "Economia!" After all, they *are* oranges. He departs, and returns with some economical hens, carried, as is usual. upside down, with their legs tied together. Other economical and uneconomical purchases having been made, we set off for home.

I ask Mac if he has had a nice day, and he says, "Splendid!" with unmistakable enthusiasm.

Gazing uncomprehendingly at Mac. B. sits down on a chair that isn't there, and Mac's perfect day is brought to a delightful finish. I have never seen any one laugh so much! At intervals during dinner he breaks out again. If we had known just what tickled Mac's sense of humor. we could have arranged to give him quite a lot of quiet fun!

B. continues with his uphill task of being sociable. On the days when Max is at the dig and the three of us are in the house, B. roams around like a lost soul. He goes into the drawing-office and talks to Mac. but. meeting with no response, he comes sadly into the office, where I am busy on the typewriter getting down to the gory details of a murder.

"Oh," says B., "you're busy?"

I say "Yes" shortly.

"Writing?" asks B.

"Yes" (more shortly).

"I thought, perhaps," says B. wistfully, "I might bring the labels and the objects in here. I shouldn't be disturbing you should I?"

I have to be firm. I explain clearly that it is quite impossible for me to get on with my dead body if a live body is moving, breathing, and in all probability talking. in the near vicinity!

Poor B. goes sadly away, condemned to work in loneliness and silence. I feel convinced that, if B. ever writes a book, he will do so most easily with a wireless and a gramophone turned on close at hand and a few conversations going on in the same room!

But when visitors arrive, either at the mound or at the house, then B. comes into his own.

Nuns, French officers, visiting archaeologists, tourists —B. is willing and competent to deal with them all.

"Here's a car stopping and some people. Shall I go down and see who they are?"

"Oh, *please* do!"

And presently the party arrives, ably shepherded, with B. chatting in any necessary language. On these occasions, as we tell him, B. is worth his weight in gold.

"Mac's not much good, is he?" says B., grinning at Mac.

"Mac," I say severely, "is no good at all. He won't even *try*."

Mac gives his gentle remote smile. . . .

Mac, we discover, has a weakness. That weakness is The Horse.

The problem of B.'s pajamas is dealt with by his dropping Mac at the mound and continuing to Kamichlie in the car. Mac wants to come home midday, and Alawi suggests that he should ride home. The Sheikh has several horses. At once Mac's face lights up. That gentle aloofness disappears. Eagerness takes its place.

From thence on, whenever there is the least excuse, Mac comes home on horseback.

"The Khwaja Mac," says Alawi, "he never speaks; he whistles. When he wants the pole-boy to go to the left, he whistles; when he wants the mason to come, he whistles; now it is for a horse he whistles!"

The matter of B.'s pajamas is still unsettled. The Customs demand the exorbitant sum of eight pounds! B. points out that the pajamas only cost two pounds a pair and refuses to pay. A most difficult situation is then created. What, the Customs demand, are they to do with the parcel? They return it to the Postmaster. He is not to give it to B., and he is not to let it leave the country! We spend several wasted days and hours going into Kamichlie and arguing the matter. The Bank Manager is called in, and the officers of the Services Spéciaux. Even a high dignitary of the Maronite Church who is visiting the Bank Manager takes a hand, looking very impressive in purple robes, an immense cross, and a large bun of hair! The wretched Postmaster, though still in pajamas, gets hardly any sleep at all! The business is rapidly becoming an International incident.

Suddenly all is settled. The douanier of Amuda arrives at our house with the parcel. The complications have been resolved: thirty shillings for the duty, *douze francs cinquante pour les timbres, et des cigarettes, n'est ce pas?* (Packets of cigarettes are pushed into his hand.) "Voilà, Monsieur!" He beams, B. beams, everybody beams. We all stand round and watch B. open his parcel.

He holds the contents up proudly, explaining, like the White Knight, that this is a special invention of his own.

"Mosquitoes," he explains. "Does away with mosquito nets."

Max says he's never seen a mosquito in these parts.

"Of course there are mosquitoes," B. says. "It is well known. Stagnant water!"

My eyes go immediately to Mac.

"There's no stagnant water here," I say. "If so, Mac would have seen it!"

B. says triumphantly that there is a pond of stagnant water just to the north of Amuda.

Max and I repeat that we have never heard or seen any mosquito. B. pays no attention, but enlarges on his invention.

The pajamas are of white washing silk. They are all in one, with a hood that comes up over the head, and the sleeves end in fingerless gloves. A zip closes up the front, so that the only parts of the wearer exposed to mosquito attack are the eyes and nose.

"And you breathe in and out through your nose, which keeps off the mosquitoes," says B. triumphantly.

Max repeats chillingly that there are no mosquitoes.

B. gives us to understand that when we are all aching and shivering with malaria we shall wish we had adopted his idea.

Mac suddenly begins to laugh. We look at him inquiringly.

"I'm thinking of that time you sat down when the chair wasn't there," says Mac, and goes away happily chuckling.

We are fast asleep that night when a terrific hullabaloo breaks out. We spring up, thinking for the moment that we are being attacked by robbers. We all rush out into the dining-room. A white figure is rushing wildly up and down, yelping and jumping about.

"Good heavens, B., what's the matter?" cries Max.

For a moment we think that B. has gone mad.

But enlightenment comes.

By some means or other a mouse has insinuated itself into the mosquito-proof pajamas. The zip has jammed.

It is daylight before we stop laughing.

Only B. is not really amused. . . .

The weather is growing hotter. All sorts of new flowers come out. I am no botanist, and do not know their names, and, frankly, do not want to know them. (What pleasure does it give you knowing what things are called?) But there are blue and mauve ones, like tiny lupins and little wild tulips; and golden ones, like marigolds and puce-colored delicate spikes of bloom. All the mounds are a riot of color. This is, indeed, the "fertile steppe." I visit the antika-room and borrow some suitably shaped pots. Mac, wishing to draw them, looks for them in vain. They are full of flowers.

Our house is rising now rapidly. The wooden centering is erected and mud-brick is being plastered on it. The effect is going to be very good. I congratulate Mac, standing beside him on the mound.

"This is a great deal better than my lavatory," I say.

The successful architect agrees. He complains, however, bitterly of his workmen, who have no idea at all, he says, of *accuracy*. I say I'm sure they haven't. Mac says bitterly that they just laugh and think it doesn't matter. I turn the talk to horses, and Mac cheers up.

With the hotter weather, our workmen's tempers grow hotter also. Max increases fines for broken heads, and at last comes to a desperate decision. Every morning the men are to hand in their weapons before they start work. It is an unpopular decision, but reluctantly the men agree. Under Max's eye, bludgeons, maces, and long murderous-looking knives are handed over to Michel, who locks them away inside Mary. At sunset they are returned to the owners. It wastes time and is tedious, but at least the workmen escape more serious damage.

A Yezidi workman comes and complains that he is faint for want of water. He cannot work unless he has water to drink.

"But there is water here—why do you not drink?"

"I cannot drink that water. It comes from the well, and this morning the Sheikh's son dropped lettuce into the well."

The Yezidis, by their religion, must never mention lettuce or touch anything contaminated by it, for they believe Shaitan resided in it.

Max says: "Now, I think that lies have been told to you. For this very morning I saw the Sheikh's son in Kamichlie, and he told me he had been there two days. This has been said to you to deceive you."

The Riot Act is then read to the assembled workmen. No one is to tell lies to or to persecute the Yezidi workmen. "On this dig all are to be brothers."

A Mohammedan with a merry eye steps forward.

"You follow Christ, Khwaja, and we follow Mohammed, but both of us are the enemies of Shaitan (the devil). Therefore it is our duty to persecute those who believe that Shaitan shall be restored and who worship him."

"Then to do your duty in future will cost you five francs a time!" says Max.

For some days after this we get no more Yezidi complaints.

The Yezidis are a curious and singularly gentle people, and their worship of Shaitan (Satan) is more in the nature of a propitiation. Moreover, they believe that this world has been placed in the charge of Shaitan by God—and to the age of Shaitan there will succed the age of Jesus, whom they recognize as a Prophet, but one not yet come to power. Shaitan's name must never be mentioned, nor any word that sounds like it.

Their holy shrine, Sheikh 'Adi, is situated in the Kurdish hills near Mosul, and we visited it when we were digging near there. There can be, I think, no spot in the world so beautiful or so peaceful. You wind up far into the hills, through oak trees and pomegranates, following a mountain stream. The air is fresh and clear and pure. You must go on foot or by horse for the last few miles of the way. Human nature is said to be so pure in these parts that the Christian woman can bathe naked in the streams.

And then, suddenly, you come to the white spires of the Shrine. All is calm gentle and peaceful there. There are trees, a courtyard, running water. Gentle-faced custodians bring you refreshments and you sit in perfect peace, sipping tea. In the Inner Court is the entrance to the Temple, on the right of which is carved a great black serpent. The snake is sacred, since the Yezidis believe that the Ark of Noah was grounded on the Jebel Sinjar and that a hole was made in it. The serpent formed itself into a coil and stopped up the hole so that the Ark could proceed.

Presently we removed our shoes and were taken into the Temple, carefully stepping over the threshold, since it is forbidden to step on a threshold. It is also

forbidden to show the soles of the feet, a slightly difficult feat when one is sitting cross-legged on the ground.

The interior is dark and cool and there is trickling
water, the sacred Spring, which is said to communi-
cate with Mecca. In this Temple the Image of the Peacock is brought at festival times. A peacock was chosen
as the representative of Shaitan, some say, because it
was the word most different from the Forbidden name.
At any rate, it is Lucifer, Son of the Morning, who
is the Peacock Angel of the Yezidi faith.

We came out again and sat in the cool silence and
peace of the court. Both of us felt loath to return from
this mountain sanctuary to the turmoil of the world. . . .

Sheikh 'Adi is a place I shall never forget—nor shall
I forget the utter peace and satisfaction that possessed
my spirit there. . . .

The head of the Yezidis, the Mir, came once to our
dig in Iraq. A tall, sad-faced man dressed all in black.
He is the Pope as well as the Chief, though local tradition had it that this particular Mir was entirely "run"
by his aunt, the Khatūn of the Shrine of Sheikh 'Adi
and his mother, a handsome ambitious woman, who
was said to keep her son under drugs so that she could
wield authority.

On a trip through the Jebel Sinjar, we paid a visit to
the Yezidi Sheikh of the Sinjar, Hâmo Shero, a very
old man, said to be ninety years of age. During the
war of 1914-18 hundreds of Armenian refugees fled
from the Turks, and were given shelter in the Sinjar and
their lives saved.

Another furious dissension breaks out over the day
of rest. The day after pay-day is always a holiday.
The Mohammedans claim that since there are more
Mohammedans than Christians on the dig, Friday
should be chosen as the day of rest. The Armenians
refuse, in any case, to work on a Sunday, and say that
as it is a Christian dig, Sunday should be the holiday.

We decree that the holiday shall always be a Tuesday, which, so far as we know, is the feast-day of no particular religion.

In the evenings the foremen come to the house, drink coffee with us, and report on the difficulties or problems that arise.

Old Abd es Salaam is particularly eloquent this evening. His voice rises in a long impassioned monologue. I cannot get the hang of it, though I listen attentively. It is, however, so very dramatic that my curiosity is aroused. When Abd es Salaam pauses for breath, I ask Max what it is all about.

Max replies in one brief word: "Constipation."

Sensing my interest, Abd es Salaam turns towards me, and pours out further rhetorical details of his condition.

Max says: "He's had Eno's, Beecham's, Vegetable laxatives, and Castor Oil. He's telling you exactly how each one has made him feel, and how none of them has brought about the desired result."

Clearly, the French doctor's horse medicine is indicated.

Max administers a terrific dose! Abd es Salaam goes hopefully away, and we all pray for a happy result!

I am now quite busy. In addition to repairing pottery, there is the photography—a "dark room" has been allotted to me. It somewhat resembles the "Little Ease" of medieval times.

In it, one can neither sit nor stand! Crawling in on all fours, I develop plates, kneeling with bent head. I come out practically asphyxiated with heat and unable to stand upright, and take a good deal of pleasure in detailing my sufferings, though the audience is somewhat inattentive—their entire interest is in the negatives, not in the operator.

Max occasionally remembers to say warmly and tactfully: "I think you're wonderful, dear," in a slightly abstracted manner.

Our house is finished. From the summit of the mound it has a holy appearance, with its great dome rising up white against the sun-baked ground. Inside, it is very pleasant. The dome gives a feeling of spaciousness and it is cool. The two rooms on one side are, first, the Antika-room, and beyond it Max's and my bedroom. On the other side is the drawing-office, and beyond a bedroom shared by B. and Mac. We shall only be here for a week or two this year. Harvest is already come, and the men leave the work every day to go and reap. The flowers are gone, vanished overnight, for the Beduin have come down from the hills, their brown tents are all round, and their cattle at pasturage eat as they go slowly south.

We shall return next year—return to our home, for this domed house in the middle of nowhere already feels like home.

The Sheikh in his snowy robes tours round it appreciatively, his merry little eyes sparkling. This is to be his inheritance eventually, and already he feels an added prestige.

It will be good to see England again. Good to see friends and green grass and tall trees. But it will be good too, to return next year.

Mac is doing a sketch. It is a sketch of the mound —a highly formalised view, but one which I admire very much.

There are no human beings to be seen; just curving lines and patterns. I realize that Mac is not only an architect. He is an artist. I ask him to design a jacket for my new book.

B. comes in, and complains that all the chairs are packed—there is nothing to sit on.

"What do you want to sit down for?" asks Max. "There's a lot of work to be done."

He goes out, and B. says reproachfully to me:

"What an energetic man your husband is!"

I wonder who would believe this if they had only seen Max asleep on a summer afternoon in England . . .?

I begin to think of Devon, of red rocks and blue sea. . . . It is lovely to be going home—my daughter, the dog, bowls of Devonshire cream, apples, bathing. . . . I draw a sigh of ecstasy.

VI

JOURNEY'S END

OUR FINDS HAVE been encouraging, and we are to continue digging for another season.

This year we shall be a different team.

Mac is with another dig in Palestine, but hopes to come to us for the last few weeks of the season.

So we shall have a different architect. There will also be an extra member of the staff—the Colonel. Max hopes to combine a certain amount of digging at Tell Brak with the Chagar dig, and the Colonel can be in charge at one dig whilst Max is at the other.

Max, the Colonel, and our new architect travel out together, and I am to follow a couple of weeks later.

About a fortnight before they start, our architect rings up and asks for Max, who is out. He sounds worried. I ask if it is anything I can do?

He says: "Well, it's just about the journey. I'm at Cook's trying to book my sleeper to the place Max told me, and Cook's say there just isn't any such place."

I reassure him.

"They often say that. Nobody ever goes to the sort

of places we do, and so, naturally, they haven't heard
of them."

"They seem to think that what I really mean is
Mosul."

"Well," I assure him "you don't."

A light dawns on me. "Did you ask for Kamichlie
or Nisibin?"

"Kamichlie! Isn't that the name of the place?"

"It's the name of the *place,* but the station is Nisibin
—it's on the Turkish side of the frontier. Kamichlie is
the Syrian town."

"That explains it. Max didn't say there was anything
else I ought to take, did he?"

"I don't think so. You've got plenty of pencils,
haven't you?"

"Pencils?" The voice sounds surprised. "Of course."

"You will need plenty of pencils," I say.

Without fully realizing the sinister significance of
this, he rings off.

My progress to Stamboul is peaceful, and I get my
quota of shoes safely past the Turkish Customs!

At Haidar Pacha I find I am to share a compartment with a large-sized Turkish lady. She has already
six suitcases, two peculiar-shaped baskets, some striped
bags, and various parcels of provisions. By the time I
have added my two suitcases and a hat-box there is
simply no room to put our legs anywhere!

Seeing the large lady off is another slimmer and more
lively lady. She addresses me in French, and we converse amiably. I am going to Alep? Ah, her cousin not
so far! Do I speak German? Her cousin speaks a little
German.

No, alas, I speak no German! And no Turkish? And
no Turkish!

How unfortunate! Her cousin speaks no French!
What, then, are we to do? How shall we be able to
converse?

It seems, I say, that we shall not be able to converse.

"A thousand pities," says the lively cousin. "It would

have been interesting for both of you. But, before the train goes, let us say all we can. You are married—yes?" I admit that I am married. "And children? You have many children, no doubt? My cousin has four children only—but," adds the cousin proudly—"three of them are boys!" I feel that for English prestige I cannot admit to being perfectly contented with one daughter. I add a couple of sons with shameless mendacity.

"Excellent!" says the cousin, beaming. "Now, as to miscarriages? How many miscarriages have you had? My cousin has had five—two at three months, two at five months, and one premature stillborn child at seven months." I am just hesitating whether to invent a miscarriage to enhance the friendly feeling when mercifully a whistle blows, and the lively cousin leaps out of the carriage and along the corridor. "You must tell each other all the details by signs," she screams.

The prospect is alarming, but we get along very well by means of nods, becks, and smiles. My companion offers me generous portions of her immense supplies of highly spiced food, and I bring her back an apple from the dining-car by way of polite rejoinder.

After the unpacking of the food baskets, there is even less room for our feet, and the smell of food and musk is almost overpowering!

When night comes, my travelling companion makes sure that the window is tightly closed. I retire to the upper berth, and wait till gentle and rhythmical snores proceed from the lower bunk.

Very stealthily I slip down and surreptitiously let down the window a fraction. I retire aloft again undiscovered.

Great pantomime of surprise in the morning when the window is discovered to be open. With multitudinous gestures the Turkish lady tries to assure me that it is not her fault. She thought she had closed it. I assure her by gesture that I do not blame her for a moment. It is, I infer, one of those things that happen.

When we reach the Turkish lady's station she parts

from me with great politeness. We smile, nod, bow, and express regret that the language bar has prevented us from really getting down to an exchange of the essential facts of life.

At lunch-time I sit opposite a kindly old American lady. She looks out reflectively at women working in the fields.

"Poor souls!" she sighs out. "I wonder if they realize that they are free!"

"Free?" I am slightly at a loss.

"Why, certainly; they don't wear the veil any longer. Mustapha Kemal has done away with all that. They're free now."

I look thoughtfully at the laboring women. It does not seem to me that the point would have any significance for them. Their day is a ceaseless round of toil, and I doubt very much if they have ever enjoyed the luxury of veiling their faces. None of our local workmen's wives do.

I do not, however, argue the point.

The American lady calls the attendant and demands a glass of hot water. *"Je vais Prendre,"* she says, *"des remèdes."*

The man looks blank. Would she like coffee, he says, or tea? With difficulty we make him understand that it is plain hot water that is required.

"You'll take some salts with me?" says my new friend matily, as one who suggests a cocktail together. I thank her, but say I don't care for salts. "But they're *good* for you," she urges. I have great difficulty in avoiding having my system drastically purged.

I retire to my carriage, and wonder how Abd es Salaam's constipation is getting on this year!

I break the journey at Alep, since there are some things Max wants me to get there. Since I have a day to spare before the next train to Nisibin, I agree to make one of a party going to motor out to Kalat Siman.

The party turns out to be a mining engineer and a very elderly and almost totally deaf clergyman. The clergyman, for some reason, takes it into his head that the mining engineer, whom I have never seen before in my life, is my husband.

"Your husband speaks Arabic very well, my dear," he remarks, patting my hand benignly as we return from our expedition.

I yell rather confusedly:

"He does, but he isn't . . ."

"Oh, yes, he is," says the clergyman reprovingly. "He is a very fine Arabic scholar."

"He isn't my husband," I shout.

"Your wife doesn't speak Arabic at all, I gather," says the clergyman, turning to the engineer, who turns brick red.

"She isn't . . ." he begins loudly.

"No," says the clergyman, "I thought she wasn't proficient in Arabic." He smiles. "You must teach her."

In unison we both shout:

"We aren't married!"

The clergyman's expression changes. He looks severe and disapproving.

"Why not?" he demands.

The mining engineer says helplessly to me: "I give it up."

We both laugh, and the clergyman's face relaxes.

"I see," he says, "you've been having your little joke with me."

The car draws up by the hotel, and he gets cautiously out, unwinding a long muffler from his white whiskers. He turns and smiles on us beneficently.

"Bless you both," he says. "I hope you have a long and happy life together!"

Triumphal arrival at Nisibin! As usual, the train halts so that there is a sheer drop of five feet between the step and a surface of sharp, loose stones! A kindly fellow-passenger leaps down and clears the stones, enabling me to jump without turning my ankle. In the distance I see Max approaching, and our chauffeur, Michel. I remember Michel's three Words of Power:

Forca, the applying of brute strength (usually with disastrous results); *Sawi Proba* and *Economia,* the general principle of Economy, which has led before now to break-down in the desert without petrol.

Before we all meet, a uniformed Turk says "Passport" sternly to me, takes it away, and leaps back upon the train.

Greetings then take place. I shake the leathery hand of Michel, who says "Bon Jour. How do you do?" And then adds in Arabic a "God-be-praised" for my safe arrival. Various underlings seize suitcases which the Wagon Lit conductor has been hurling out of the windows. I mention my passport. It and the uniformed Turk have completely disappeared.

Blue Mary—our lorry—is waiting faithfully. Michel opens the back door, and a familiar sight meets the eyes. Several hens, uncomfortably tied together; tins of benzine and heaps of sacking that eventually turn out to be human beings. My luggage is stowed on top of the hens, and the humans and Michel depart to seek my passport. Fearing that Michel may apply *Forca* and create an international complication, Max goes after him. After twenty minutes or so they return triumphant.

We start off—creak, lurch, rattle, bound in and out of potholes. We pass from Turkey into Syria. Five minutes later we are in that rising township of Kamichlie.

There is much business afoot before we can set out for home. We proceed first to "Harrods"—namely, the establishment of M. Yannakos. Here I receive greetings, am offered the chair behind the till, and coffee is brewed for me. Michel is completing the purchase of a horse, which is to be attached to a cart and carry water from the river Jaghjagha to our excavations on Tell Brak. Michel has found, so he says, an excellent horse—a horse extremely *economia.* "How economia is the horse?" Max asks suspiciously. "Is it a good horse? A large horse? A horse of endurance? Better," he says, "a good horse costing a little more money than an inferior horse at a cheap price."

One of the bundles of sacking has left the lorry and turns out to be the ruffian who is to be the waterman —a man with (so he says) a knowledge of horses. He is to go with Michel and report on the horse. Meanwhile we buy tinned fruits, bottles of doubtful wine, macaroni, pots of plum and apple jam, and other delicacies, from M. Yannakos. We then proceed to the Post Office, where we find our old friend the unshaven Postmaster in dirty pajamas. The pajamas do not appear to have been washed or changed since last year. We take our bundles of newspapers and a letter or two, reject three other letters addressed in European handwriting to a Mr. Thompson, which the Postmaster presses anxiously upon us, and go on to the bank.

The Bank is of stone—large, cool, empty, very peaceful. There is a bench in the middle, on which sit two soldiers, an old man in picturesque colored rags with a hennaed beard, and a boy in torn European clothing. They all sit peacefully gazing into space and occasionally spitting. There is a mysterious bed with dingy blankets in a corner. We are received with pleasure by the clerk behind the counter. Max produces a check to be cashed, and we are shown into the office of M. le Directeur. M. le Directeur is large, coffee colored, and voluble. He receives us with the utmost amiability. Coffee is sent for. He has replaced the *directeur* of last year, and is rather sad about it. He has come from Alexandretta, where, as he says, there is a *little* life! But here (his hands fly up), *"On ne peut même pas faire un Bridge!"* "No," he adds, his sense of injury growing, *"pas même un tout petit Bridge."* (Note—what is the difference between *un Bridge* and *un tout petit Bridge?* Presumably both need four players?)

Half an hour passes in conversation on the political situation, and the amenities (or lack of them) in Kamichlie. *"Mais tout de même on fait des belles constructions,"* he admits. He is living, it appears, in one of these new constructions. One has not the electric light, the sanitation, nor any civilized comforts, but the house is at least a *construction*—*"une construction en pierre, vous comprenez!* Madame will see it on her way to Chagar Bazar."

I promise to look out for it.

We discuss the local Sheikhs. They are all alike, he says. *"Des propriétaires—mais qui n'ont pas le sou!"* They are always in debt.

At intervals during the conversation the cashier enters with five or six forms, which Max signs, and also disburses small sums, such as sixty centimes *pour les timbres*.

The coffee comes, and after forty minutes the little cashier arrives with the last three documents, a final request of *"Et deux francs quarante cinq centimes pour les timbres, s'il vous plaît,"* and it is intimated that the final ceremonies have been completed, and that the money can now be handed over. *"C'est à dire, si nous avons de l'argent ici!"*

Coldly, Max points out that he has given notice of his intention to draw a check a week previously. The cashier shrugs his shoulders, smiling. "Ah well, we will see!" Fortunately all is well, the money is forthcoming, *les timbres* are affixed, we can leave. The same people are sitting on the benches, still gazing into space and spitting.

We return to Harrods. The Kurdish waterman is waiting for us. He reports that Michel's horse—well, one cannot call it a horse! It is not a horse at all. It is an old woman—just that; an old woman! So much for Michel's *economia*. Max goes to inspect the horse, and I return to the chair behind the till.

M. Yannakos Junior entertains me with halting conversation on the events of the great world. *"Votre roi,"* he says. *"Votre roi—vous avez un nouveau roi."* I agree that we have a new King. M. Yannakos struggles to express thoughts that go beyond his words. *"Le Roi d'angleterre!"* he says. *"Grand roi—Plus grand roi dans tout monde—aller—comme ça."* He makes an ex-

pressive gesture. *"Pour une femme!"* It is beyond him.
"Pour une femme!" No, such a thing is not believable.
Is it possible that such an extraordinary importance attaches to women in England? *"Le plus grand roi au
monde,"* he repeats in awestruck tones.

Max, the Kurd, and Michel return. Michel, momen-
tarily cast down by the vote of censure on his horse,
has recovered all his aplomb. They are now going to
enter into negotiations for a *mule*. Michel murmurs
that a mule will be very expensive. The Kurd says that
a mule is always valuable. The Kurd and Michel go off
in search of a man whose second cousin's husband
knows a man who has a mule to sell.

Sudden appearance of our idiot houseboy, Mansur.
He beams welcome and shakes me warmly by the hand.
He it is whom it took one whole season to teach to
lay the table—and even now he is apt to break out into
an eruption of forks for tea. Making the beds strains
his mental capacity to the utmost. His movements are
slow, dogged, and everything he does is in the nature
of a trick successfully taught to a dog.

Will we come to the house of his mother (who, incidentally, does our washing) and inspect a collection
of antikas?

We go. The room is much swept and garnished.
For the third time in two hours I drink coffee. The
antikas are brought out—little Roman glass bottles,
fragments of glaze and pottery, odd coins, and a good
deal of complete junk. Max divides it into two groups,
rejecting one, offering his price for the other. A woman
enters, who is clearly an interested party. It seems a
moot point whether she will complete the sale or have
twins first. By the aspect of her it might even be quins.
She listens to Mansur's translations, shakes her head.

We leave and return to the lorry. Negotiations for
the mule having been begun, we go to inspect the
water-barrels, which are to be transported in the cart
the mule is to draw. Once more Michel is in trouble.
He has ordered one water-barrel of such immense
dimensions that it would not fit in the cart, and would

probably kill any horse or mule. "But," wails Michel, "one big water-barrel is more *economia* to make than two small ones, and it holds more water!" Michel is told he is a blasted fool, and that in future he is to do as he is told. He murmurs hopefully: "Sawi proba?" but even that hope is dashed from him.

Next we meet the Sheikh—our own particular Sheikh. He is looking more than ever like Henry the Eighth, with his immense henna-dyed beard. He wears his usual white robes, and an emerald green cloth wound round his head. He is in an extremely jovial mood, as he proposes shortly to visit Baghdad, though, of course, it will take many weeks before his passport is arranged. "Brother," he says to Max, "everything that I have is yours. For your sake, I have not sown any seed in the ground this year that all the land might be at your disposal." My husband replies: "How happy I am that such nobility has also turned out to your own advantage. This year all crops are failing. Those who have sown seed will lose money. You are to be congratulated on your acumen."

Honor thus satisfied, they part on the best of terms.

We climb into Blue Mary. Michel dumps a load of potatoes and oranges on top of my hat-box, completely denting it in; the hens squawk; several Arabs and Kurds beg for conveyance—two are accepted. They get in among the hens and the potatoes and the luggage, and off we go to Chagar Bazar.

VII

LIFE AT CHAGAR BAZAR

WITH AN IMMENSE wave of excitement I catch sight of
Our House. There it stands, with its dome, looking like
a shrine dedicated to some venerable saint!

The Sheikh, Max tells me, is intensely proud of it.
At intervals he and his friends circle round it admiringly, and Max suspects that he is already raising
money on it by falsely representing that it belongs to
him, and is merely rented to us.

Mary draws up with Michel's usual violent application of the brakes *(Forca),* and everyone rushes out of
the house to greet us. There are old faces and new
ones.

Dimitri, the cook, is the same. His long, gentle face
is definitely maternal. He is wearing long trousers of
flowered muslin and beaming with pleasure. He seizes
my hand and presses it against his forehead, then
proudly displays a wooden box with four new-born
puppies in it. These, he says, will be our future watch-
dogs. Ali, the boy, was also with us last year. He is
now feeling rather superior, as a second and lesser

cook's boy is now employed, by name Ferhid. There is little to say about Ferhid, except that he looks worried about something. But this, Max informs me, is Ferhid's chronic condition.

We have also a new house-boy—Subri. Subri is tall and fierce and looks very intelligent. He grins and shows teeth of assorted white and gold.

The Colonel and Bumps have tea ready for us. The Colonel does things with military precision. Already he has instituted a new custom of lining up the men in military formation at bakshish-time. They think it a great joke. He spends a lot of time tidying up. The days when Max goes into Kamichlie are his great opportunity. The house, he announces proudly, is now as neat as a new pin. Everything that has a place is in its place, and quite a lot of things that have not got a place have been found a place! So much so, that all kinds of inconvenience will arise!

Bumps is our new architect. His nickname has arisen out of an innocent remark made by him to the Colonel on the journey out. In the early dawn, as the train was approaching Nisibin, Bumps pulled up the blind and looked out with interest on the country where the next few months of his life were to be spent.

"Curious place this is," he remarks. "It's all over *bumps!*"

"Bumps, indeed!" cries the Colonel. "Don't you realize, you irreverent fellow, that each of those *bumps* is a buried city dating back thousands of years?"

And from henceforth Bumps is to be our new colleague's name!

There are other new acquisitions for me to see. First, a second-hand Citröen, which the Colonel has christened Poilu.

Poilu turns out to be a very temperamental gentleman. For some reason or other he always chooses the Colonel with whom to misbehave, obstinately refusing to start, or else staging a break-down at some inconvenient spot.

The solution of this mystery dawns on me one day, and I explain to the Colonel that it is his fault.

"How do you mean—*my* fault?"

"You shouldn't have christened him Poilu. After all, if our lorry started as Queen Mary, the least you could do was to christen the Citröen the Empress Josephine. If so, you'd have had no trouble!"

The Colonel, like the disciplinarian he is, says that at any rate it is too late now. Poilu is Poilu, and will have to behave himself. I look sideways at Poilu, who seems to be regarding the Colonel with a rakish air. Poilu, I feel sure, is contemplating that most serious of military crimes—mutiny!

The foremen next come rushing up to greet me. Yahya looks more than ever like a great happy dog. Alawi is looking, as always, very handsome. Old Abd es Salaam is, as usual, full of conversation.

I ask Max how Abd es Salaam's constipation is, and Max replies that most evenings have been devoted to the exhaustive discussion of it!

Then we go to the Antika-room. The first work period of ten days is just concluded, with the bumper result of a find of nearly a hundred tablets, so everyone is very jubilant. In another week we are starting to dig at Tell Brak as well as Chagar.

Back in the house at Chagar, it seems as though I had never been away, though, owing to the Colonel's passion for order, the house is looking a good deal tidier than I have ever seen it. Which brings me to the sad story of the Camembert cheeses.

Six Camembert cheeses had been bought by Max in Alep under the impression that you can treat a Camembert cheese like a Dutch cheese and store it away until wanted. One had been eaten before my arrival, and the Colonel, coming across the other five in his tidying round, had stacked them neatly at the back of a cupboard in the living-room. There they were rapidly overlaid by drawing-paper, typewriting-paper, cigarettes, Turkish delight, etc., and languished in darkness—unremembered, unseen, but not, let it be said, *unsmelt.*

A fortnight later we are all sniffing and hazarding guesses.

"If I didn't know that we'd *got* no drains—" says Max.

"And the nearest gas-pipe must be about two hundred miles away—"

"So I suppose it *must* be a dead mouse."

"A dead rat at least!"

Life indoors becoming unendurable, a determined search is made for the hypothetical disintegrating rat. Then, and only then, is the discovery made of a gluey odorous mass which has once been five Camembert cheeses, and which, passing through the *coulant* stage, are now *coulant* to the *n*th degree.

Accusing eyes are turned on the Colonel, and the horrible remains are entrusted to Mansur for solemn burial at a spot remote from the house. Max explains to the Colonel with feeling how this confirms what he has always known—that the idea of tidiness is a great mistake! The Colonel explains that the tidying away of the cheeses was a good idea; the fault lies in the absent-mindedness of archaeologists who cannot remember that they have Camembert cheeses in the house. I explain that the real mistake lies in buying ripe Camembert cheeses *en bloc* to store for the season! Bumps says, why buy Camembert cheeses, anyway? *He* has never liked them! Mansur takes away the horrible remains and buries them obediently, but he is, as usual, puzzled. Presumably the Khwajas *like* these things, since they pay good money for them? Why, then, destroy them, when their good qualities have become so much more evident than they were before? Obviously it is all a part and parcel of the extraordinary ways of employers!

The servant problem on the Habur is very different from the servant problem in England. You might say that here the servants have an employer problem! Our fancies, prejudices, likes and dislikes are quite fantastic, and follow, to the native mind, no logical pattern whatever!

For instance, various cloths of slightly different texture with different colored borders are issued, and are supposed to be used for different purposes. Why this elaboration?

Why, when Mansur is using a blue-edged teacloth to wipe mud from the car's radiator, does an incensed Khatūn emerge from the house full of condemnation? The cloth has removed the mud most successfully. Again, why unmerited censure when a visit to the kitchen reveals the fact that the breakfast things after washing up are being wiped with a sheet?

"But," protests Mansur, anxious to vindicate his conduct, "it is not a clean sheet we are using. It is a dirty sheet!"

Incomprehensibly this seems to make matters worse.

In the same way civilization's invention of table cutlery presents a perpetual headache to a worried houseboy.

More than once I have watched through an open doorway Mansur nerving himself to the task of laying the table for lunch.

First he adjusts the tablecloth—very seriously trying it both ways, and standing well back to observe which effect is the more pleasing artistically.

Inevitably he plumps for the length of the cloth being placed across the table, so that there is a graceful fall on either side and the ends of the table show an inch of two of bare board. He nods approval, and then, a frown gathering on his forehead, he peers into a somewhat moth-eaten plate basket, bought cheap in Beyrout, in which reposes assorted cutlery.

Here is the real problem. Carefully, and with every sign of mental strain, he places a fork on each cup and saucer and a knife to the left of each plate. He stands back, and studies the effect with his head on one side. He shakes his head and sighs. Something seems to tell him that that is the wrong arrangement. Something also seems to tell him that never, not even at the

end of the season, will he really have mastered the
principle behind the varied combinations of those three
units—knife, fork, and spoon. Even at tea, the simplest
meal, his arrangement of a single fork does not meet
with favor. For some inscrutable reason we demand,
at a time when there is nothing serious to cut, a knife!
It simply does not make sense.

With a deep sigh Mansur proceeds with his complicated task. To-day, at least, he is determined to
please. He looks again. He lays a couple of forks to
the right of every plate, and adds a spoon or knife at
alternate places. Breathing heavily, he places plates
in position, bends and blows on them ferociously to
remove any adherent dust. Tottering slightly with the
intense mental strain, he leaves the room to inform
the cook that all is in readiness, and that the latter can
now remove the omelette from the oven, where it has
been keeping hot and getting nice and leathery during
the last twenty minutes.

Ferhid, the boy, is then sent out to us. He arrives
with a worried look, as though to announce some
major catastrophe, so that it is quite a relief when all
he has to say is that dinner is ready.

To-night we have all the dishes that Dimitri considers most high class. We start with hors d'oeuvre,
hard-boiled eggs smothered in rich mayonnaise, sar-
dines, cold string beans, and anchovies. Then we have
Dimitri's specialty—a shoulder (?) of mutton stuffed
with rice, raisins, and spice. It is all very mysterious.
There is a long stitching of cotton which you have to
cut. After that, quantities of the stuffing are easily
obtained, but the actual meat eludes one, and only at
the close of the course does one, on suddenly turning
over the joint, discover the actual mutton! After that
we have pears from a tin, as Dimitri is forbidden to
make the only sweet he knows, which we all dislike—
namely, carmel custard. After this, the Colonel proudly
announces that he has taught Dimitri to make a savory.

Plates are handed round. On them is a small strip
of Arab bread smothered in hot grease, which tastes

faintly of cheese. We tell the Colonel we do not think much of his savory!

Turkish delight and some delicious preserved fruits from Damascus are then placed on the table, and at this moment the Sheikh arrives to pay us an evening call. Our decision to dig at Chagar has changed his position from one of hopeless bankruptcy to that of a man on whom a shower of gold may descend at any minute. According to the foremen, he has acquired a new and handsome Yezidi wife on the strength of this, and has increased his debts enormously as a result of enlarged credit! He is certainly in very good spirits. As always, he is armed to the teeth. Carelessly casting off his rifle and slinging it into a corner, he expatiates on the merits of an automatic pistol he has just acquired.

"See," he says, pointing it full at the Colonel. "The mechanism is like this—excellent and simple. You place your finger on the trigger—so—and bullet after bullet comes out."

In an agonized voice the Colonel asks if the pistol is loaded.

Naturally it is loaded, the Sheikh replies in a surprised voice. What would be the good of a pistol that was not loaded?

The Colonel, who has a proper military horror of loaded weapons being pointed at him, promptly changes his seat, and Max distracts the Sheikh from his new toy by offering him Turkish delight. The Sheikh helps himself lavishly, sucks his fingers in appreciation, and beams round at us all.

"Ah," he says—noting that I am engaged on *The Times* crossword puzzle—"so your Khatūn reads? Does she also write?"

Max says that such is the case.

"A very learned Khatūn," says the Sheikh appreciatively. "And does she give medicine to women? If so, my wives shall come one evening and explain to her all that ails them."

Max replies that the Sheikh's wives will be welcome,

but that his Khatūn, unfortunately, does not understand much Arabic.

"We shall manage—we shall manage," says the Sheikh cheerfully.

Mac inquires about the Sheikh's journey to Baghdad.

"It is not yet arranged," says the Sheikh. "There are difficulties—formalities."

We all have a shrewd suspicion that the difficulties are financial. Rumor has it that the Sheikh has already spent all the money he has received from us, in addition to the rake-off he has obtained from the workmen of his village.

"In the days of El Baron . . ." he begins.

But before an advance in gold can be mentioned, Max quickly circumvents him by asking where is the official receipt for the sixty Syrian pounds that the Sheikh has already received. "The Government will require it."

The Sheikh quickly gives up the idea of a touch, and explains that he has a dear friend and relation outside who has a bad eye. Will we come out and look at it and advise?

We go out into the night and look at the eye by the aid of a torch. It is certainly beyond us, being a mere gory mess. Such an eye must be seen by a doctor, says Max. As soon as possible, he adds.

The Sheikh nods. His friend is going into Alep. Will we give him a letter to Dr. Altounyan there? Max agrees, and starts upon it then and there, looking up to ask; "This man is a relation of yours, you say?"

"Yes."

"And his name?" says Max, still writing.

"His name?" The Sheikh is a little taken aback. "I do not know. I must ask him."

The Sheikh departs into the night once more, returning with the information that his relation's name is Mahmoud Hassan.

"Mahmoud Hassan," says Max, writing it down.

"Or is it," asks the Sheikh, "his *passport* name that you require? His passport name is Daoud Suliman."

Max looks puzzled, and asks what the man's name really *is?*

"Call him what you like," says the Sheikh generously.

The letter is handed over, the Sheikh resumes his warlike accoutrements, blesses us cheerfully, and departs with his mysterious follower into the night.

The Colonel and Bumps start an argument *re* King Edward the Eighth and Mrs. Simpson. This is followed by one on the subject of matrimony generally, which seems to lead quite naturally to the subject of suicide!

At this point I leave them to it and go to bed.

A high wind this morning. It rises, until about midday there is practically a dust-storm. Bumps, who has come up to the mound in a topee, has a good deal of trouble with it in the howling wind, and it finally gets entangled round his neck. Michel, always helpful, comes to the rescue.

"*Forca,*" he says, pulling hard upon a strap.

Bumps turns purple in the face as he is slowly being strangled.

"*Beaucoup forca,*" says Michel cheerfully, pulling harder, and Bumps goes black. He is rescued just in time!

A violent quarrel breaks out after the work between the hot-tempered Alawi and Serkis, our carpenter. It arises, as usual, out of nothing at all, but reaches murderous heights.

Max perforce has to administer one of what he calls his "Prep. school talks." Every day, he says, he becomes more and more fitted to be a headmaster, so easily do nauseatingly moral sentiments pour from him!

The harangue is very impressive.

"Do you imagine," demands Max, "that I and the Khwaja Colonel, and the Khwaja of the Pole, always have but a single thought in our minds? That we never wish to disagree? But do we raise our voices, shout, draw knives? No! All these things we put behind us until we go back to London! Here we put the Work first. Always the Work! We exercise control!"

Alawi and Serkis are deeply affected, the quarrel is made up, and their touching politeness to each other as to who should pass out of the door first is really beautiful to behold!

Purchase has been made of a bicycle—an extremely cheap Japanese bicycle. This is to be the proud possession of the boy Ali, and on it he is to ride into Kamichlie two days a week and collect the post.

He sets out, full of importance and happiness, at daybreak, returning about tea-time.

I say doubtfully to Max that it is a long way to go. Kamichlie is forty kilometers away. I do rather sketchy sums in my head, and murmur: "Twenty-five miles, and twenty-four miles back," and add in consternation: "The boy can't possibly do that. It's far too much for him."

Max says (callously in my opinion): "Oh, I don't think so!"

"He must be exhausted," I murmur. I leave the room, and go in search of the overworked Ali. No sign of him.

Dimitri at last understands what I am talking about.

"Ali? Ali has come back from Kamichlie half an hour ago. Where is he now? He has bicycled to the village of Germayir, eight kilometers away, where he has a friend."

My solicitude on Ali's behalf is abruptly damped, especially when he assists with waiting at table at dinnertime with a radiant face and no signs of fatigue.

Max jeers and murmurs cryptically: "Remember Swiss Miss?"

I fall to thinking of Swiss Miss and her times.

Swiss Miss was one of five mongrel puppies on our first dig at Arpachiyah, near Mosul. They rejoiced (or acquiesced) in the names of Woolly Boy, Boujy, Whitefang, Tomboy, and Swiss Miss. Boujy died young of a surfeit of *klechah* which is a form of exceptionally heavy pastry eaten by Christian sects at Easter. Some was brought to us by our Christian foremen and became somewhat of an embarrassment. Having suffered from its effects ourselves and seriously upset the digestion of an innocent girl guest who partook of it heartily for tea, we surreptitiously fed the remainder of it to Boujy. Boujy, unbelievingly crawling out into the sun, gulped this rich nourishment and promptly died! It was a death in ecstasy—and much to be envied! Of the remaining dogs, Swiss Miss was chief, since she was the Master's Favorite. She would come to Max at sunset when the work was finished, and he would industriously detick her. After that the dogs would line up by the cookhouse, Swiss Miss at their head, and when their names were called they would advance one by one to receive dinner.

Then, in some adventure, Swiss Miss broke a leg and came limping back a very sick dog. She did not die, however. When the time came for us to leave, the fate of Swiss Miss weighed heavily upon me. Lame as she was, how would she survive once we had gone away? The only thing to do, I argued, was to have her put away. We could not leave her to die of starvation. Max, however, would not hear of this. He assured me optimistically that Swiss Miss would be all right. The others—yes, possibly, I said, they could fend for themselves, but Swiss Miss was a cripple.

The argument went on, getting more impassioned on either side. In the end, Max won and we left, pressing money into the old gardener's hand and bidding him "look after the dogs, especially Swiss Miss," but without much hope that he would do so. Fears as to Swiss Miss's fate haunted me off and on for the next two years, and I constantly reproached myself for not standing firm. When we next passed through Mosul we went out to our old house to look around. It was empty—there was no sign of life anywhere. I murmured softly to Max: "I wonder what became of Swiss Miss?"

And then we heard a growl. Sitting on the steps was

a dog—a very hideous dog (even as a puppy Swiss Miss had been no beauty). It got up, and I saw that it walked lame. We called Swiss Miss, and its tail wagged faintly, although it continued to growl under its breath. And then, from the bushes, came a small puppy, that ran to its mother. Swiss Miss must have found a handsome husband, for the puppy was a most attractive little dog. Mother and child regarded us placidly, though without real recognition.

"You see," said Max triumphantly, "I told you she'd be all right. Why, she's quite fat. Swiss Miss has brains, so, of course, she's survived. Think what a good time she'd have missed if we'd had her put away!"

Since then, when I start indulging in anxieties, the words Swiss Miss are used to quell my objections!

The mule has not been purchased after all. Instead, a horse—a real horse, not an old woman, but a grand horse, a prince among horses—has been purchased. And with the horse, inseparable from it, apparently, has come a Circassian.

"What a man!" says Michel, his voice rising in a high whine of admiration. "The Circassians know all about horses. They live for horses. And what care, what forethought this man has for his horse! He worries unceasingly about its comfort. And how polite he is! What good manners he has—to *Me!*"

Max remains unimpressed, remarking that time will show whether the man is any good. He is presented to us. He has a gay air and high boots, and reminds me of something out of a Russsian ballet.

To-day we have a visit from a French colleague—from Mari. With him came his architect. Like many French architects, he looks rather like an inferior saint. He has one of those weak nondescript beards. He says nothing but *"Merci, Madame,"* in polite negatives when offered anything. M. Parrot explains that he is suffering with his stomach.

After a pleasant visit they go off again. We admire their car. M. Parrot says sadly: *"Oui, c'est une bonne*

machine, mais elle va trop vite. Beaucoup trop vite."
He adds: "*L'année dernière elle a tué deux de mes architectes!*"

They then get in, the saintlike architect takes the wheel, and they suddenly depart in a whirl of dust at sixty miles an hour—through potholes, over bumps, twisting through the Kurdish village. It seems quite likely that yet another architect, undeterred by his predecessor's fate, will fall a victim to the determined speed of the machine. Clearly the automobile is always to blame! Never the man whose foot is on the accelerator.

The French Army is now on maneuvers. This is thrilling for the Colonel, whose martial interest is at once awakened. His eager overtures are, however, received extremely coldly by the officers to whom they are addressed. They regard him with suspicion.

I tell him that they think he is a spy.

"A spy? Me?" demands the Colonel, highly indignant. "How could they think such a thing?"

"Well, obviously they do."

"I was just asking them a few simple questions. These things are interesting technically. But their replies are so vague."

It is all very disappointing for the poor Colonel, yearning to talk shop and being firmly rebuffed.

The maneuvers worry our workmen in quite another way. One grave, bearded man comes up to Max.

"Khwaja, will the '*asker* interfere with my trade?"

"No, certainly not; they won't interfere with the dig at all."

"I do not mean the work, Khwaja, but with my own trade."

Max asks him what his trade is, and he replies proudly that it is smuggling cigarettes!

The smuggling of cigarettes over the Iraq border appears to be almost an exact science. The Customs' car arrives at a village one day—and on the next the smugglers. . . . Max asks if the Customs never turn

back and visit a village a second time. The man looks
reproachful, and says of course not. If they did, everything would go wrong. As it is, the workmen happily
smoke cigarettes that have cost them twopence a hundred!

Max questions some of the men as to what exactly
it costs them to live. Most of them bring a sack of
flour with them if they have come from a distant village.
This lasts them about ten days. Someone in the village
makes their bread for them, as apparently it is below
their dignity to bake their own. They have onions occasionally, sometimes some rice, and they probably get
sour milk. After working prices out, we find that it
costs each man about twopence a week!

Two workmen who are Turks now come up, and
in their turn ask anxiously about the *'asker.*

"Will they make trouble for *us,* Khwaja?"

"Why should they make trouble for you?"

Apparently the Turks have no business to be across
the border. One of our pickmen reassures them, however. "It will be all right," he says; "you wear the
kefiyaed."

A cap on the head is only worn uneasily in this part
of the world, and yells of derision come from the
kefiyaed Arabs and Kurds as they point a scornful
finger and yell "Turki! Turki!" at the unfortunate man,
who, by order of Mustapha Kemal, is wearing European headgear. "Uneasy lies the head that wears a
cap" in these parts.

To-night, as we finish dinner, the anxious Ferhid
comes in, and in tones of despair announces that the
Sheikh has brought his wives to ask advice of the Khatūn.

I feel slightly nervous. Apparently I have gained
quite a reputation for medical wisdom. This is singularly undeserved. Although the Kurdish women make no
bones about describing their ailments in detail to Max
to pass on to me, the more modest Arab women will
only come to me when I am alone. The scene that ensues is mostly pantomime. Headaches are fairly easily

indicated, and an aspirin accepted with reverent awe.
Bad and inflamed eyes can be seen, though to explain
the uses of boracic is more difficult.

"Mai harr," I say (Hot water).

"Mai harr," they repeat.

Then I demonstrate with a pinch of boracic—"Mithl
hadha."

Final pantomime of the bathing of eyes.

The patient then responds by a pantomime of drinking a copious draught. I shake my head. *Outward* application —to the *eyes*. The patient is a little disappointed. However, we hear next day from the foreman
that the wife of Abu Suleiman has been greatly bene-
fited by the Khatūn's medicine. She bathed her eyes
with it, and then drank it all, every drop!

The commonest gesture is an expressive rubbing of
the abdomen.

This has one of two meanings—(*a*) acute indigestion;
(*b*) a complaint of sterility.

Bicarbonate of soda does excellent work in the first
case and has attained a somewhat surprising reputation in the second.

"Your Khatūn's white powder was a worker of mar-
vels last season! I now have two strong sons—twins!"

Reviewing these past triumphs, I nevertheless shrink
a little from the ordeal in front of me. Max encourages
me with his usual optimism. The Sheikh has told him
that his wife suffers from her eyes. It will be a straight-
forward case of boracic.

The Sheikh's wives, of course, unlike the village
women, are veiled. Therefore, a lamp is taken to a
little empty storehouse, where I am to see the patient.

The Colonel and Bumps make several ribald remarks,
and do their best to rattle me as I go apprehensively
to the consulting-room.

Outside in the night about eighteen people are standing. The Sheikh greets Max with a cheerful roar, and
waves his hand towards a tall, veiled figure.

I utter the conventional greetings, and lead the way

into the little storehouse. Not one woman, but five, follow me in. They are all very excited, laughing and talking.

The door is shut upon us. Max and the Sheikh remain outside the door to do what interpretation shall be necessary.

I am a little dazed by seeing so many women. Are they *all* wives? And do they *all* need medical attention?

Off come the veils. One woman is young and tall—very handsome. I imagine that she is the new Yezidi wife just acquired with the advance rent for the land. The principal wife is much older; she looks about forty-five and is probably thirty. All the women are wearing jewelry, and all are the gay handsome Kurdish type.

The middle-aged woman points to her eyes and clasps her face. Alas, it is not a case for boracic! She is suffering, I should say, from some virulent form of blood-poisoning.

I raise my voice and speak to Max. It is a poisoning, I say, of the blood, and she should go to a doctor or a hospital in Der-ez-Zor or Alep, where she would have proper injections.

Max passes this on to the Sheikh, who appears much struck by the diagnosis. Presently Max calls out:

"He is much impressed by your cleverness. This is exactly what he has already been told by a doctor in Baghdad. He, too, said that she should have *'des piqures.'* Now that you, too, say so, the Sheikh is going seriously to consider it. By and by he will certainly take his wife to Alep."

I say that it would be a good thing if he took her soon.

This summer, says the Sheikh, or at any rate in the autumn. There is no hurry. All will be as Allah directs.

The lesser wives or whatnots are now examining my clothing in an ecstasy of delighted merriment. I give the patient some aspirin tablets to relieve pain, and recommend applications of hot water, etc. She is far more interested, however, in my appearance than in her own condition. I offer Turkish delight and we all laugh and smile and pat each other's clothes.

Finally, regretfully, the women resume their veils and take their leave. I return, a nervous wreck, to the living-room.

I ask Max whether he thinks the Sheikh will take her to hospital somewhere and Max says probably not.

Today Michel goes into Kamichlie with the washing, and a long list of shopping to be done. Michel cannot read or write, but he never forgets an item, and can recall its exact price. He is scrupulously honest, which offsets his many annoying qualities. I myself would list the latter in the following order:

1. His high whining voice.
2. His tendency to beat "tutti" under one's window.
3. His hopeful attempts to murder Moslems on the road.
4. His argumentative powers.

A lot of photography to-day, and I am introduced to my "dark room." This is undoubtedly a great improvement on the "Little Ease" at Amuda. I can stand upright, and it has a table and a chair.

But as it is a recent addition, having been added a few days before my arrival, the mud-brick is still damp. Strange fungi grow on the walls, and when one is immured in it on a hot day, one comes out partially asphyxiated!

Max has given the little boy who sits outside and washes the pottery a bar of chocolate, and tonight the little boy waylays him.

"Tell me, I pray you, Khwaja, the name of that sweetmeat? So delicious is it that I no longer care for the sweets of the Bazaar. I must purchase this new sweetmeat, even if it's price should be a mejidi!"

I say to Max that he must feel as though he has created a drug addict. Clearly, chocolate is habit-forming.

Not, Max remarks, like an old man to whom he once offered a piece of chocolate last year. The old man thanked him courteously and folded it away in his robe. The officious Michel asked if he were not going to eat it. "It is good," said Michel. The old man replied simply: "It is *new*. It might be dangerous!"

Today is our day off, and we go over to Brak to make arrangements there. The mound itself is about a mile from Jaghjaga, and the first question to be solved is the water problem. We have had a local well-digger at work, but the water by the mound has proved too brackish for drinking. It will have, therefore, to be brought up from the river—hence the Circassian, the cart, and the water-barrels (and the horse that is not an old woman). We shall also need a watchman to live on the excavations.

For ourselves, we are renting a house in the Armenian village by the river. Most of the houses are deserted there. The settlement began with a considerable expenditure of money, but, so far as one can judge, without the necessary putting of first things first. The houses (miserable mudbrick hovels, though they would probably appear to the Western eye!) were actually overambitious, bigger and more elaborate than was needful, whereas the water-wheel on which the irrigation and the whole success of the settlement depended was scamped, since there was not enough money left to build it really well. The settlement was started on a kind of communal basis. Tools, animals, ploughs, etc., were provided, and were to be paid off by the community out of their profits. What actually happened, however, was that one after another tired of life in the wilds, and wished to return to a city, and departed, taking his tools and implements with him. Result: These had continually to be replaced, and the people who remained and worked became, much to their bewilderment, more and more in debt. The water-wheel finally failed to function, and the settlement relapsed into a mere village—and a somewhat disgruntled village at that. The derelict house that we are renting is quite imposing, with a wall round a courtyard, and actually a two-storied "tower" on one side. Facing the tower on the other side is a line of rooms, each opening on to the courtyard. Serkis, the carpenter, is busy now repairing the woodwork of doors and windows, so that a few of the rooms will be habitable to camp in.

Michel is dispatched to collect the new watchman for the mound from a village a couple of miles away, together with a tent.

Serkis reports that the tower-room is the one in the best order. We go up some steps, across a small flat roof, and then into two rooms. We agree that the inner room shall have a couple of camp-beds in it, and that the outer one will do for meals, etc. There are some hinged wooden boards to swing-to across the windows, but Serkis will fit some glass.

Michel now returns, and reports that the watchman he has been sent to transport to the mound has three wives, eight children, many sacks of flour and rice, and a good deal of livestock. Impossible to transport them all in the lorry. What shall he do?

He departs again with three Syrian pounds and instructions to bring what he can, and the surplus can hire themselves passages on donkeys.

The Circassian appears suddenly, driving the water-cart. He is singing and shaking a large whip. The cart is painted a bright blue and yellow, the water-barrels are blue, the Circassian has high boots and gay wrappings. The whole think looks more like the Russian ballet than ever. The Circassian descends, cracks his whip and continues to sing, swaying on his feet. He is clearly very drunk!

Another of Michel's swans!

The Circassian is sacked, and one Abdul Hassan, a serious melancholy man, who says he understands horses, is appointed in his stead.

We start home, and run out of petrol two miles from Chagar. Max turns on Michel with fury and curses him.

Michel raises his hands to heaven and lets out a wail of injured innocence.

It is entirely in our interests that he has acted. He has wished to utilize the very last drop of petrol.

"You fool! Haven't I told you always to fill up *and* carry a spare can?"

"There would have been no room for a spare can, and, besides, it might have been stolen."

"And why didn't you fill up the tank?"

"I wished to see just how far the car would go on what we had."

"Idiot!"

Michel says appeasingly: "Sawi proba," which rouses Max to a howl of fury. We all feel inclined to apply *Forca* to Michel, as he continues to look virtuous—an innocent man unjustly blamed!

Max restrains himself, but says that he sees why Armenians are massacred!

We arrive home at last, to be greeted by Ferhid, stating he wishes to "retire," as he and Ali never stop quarrelling!

VIII

CHAGAR AND BRAK

THERE ARE PENALTIES attached to greatness. Of our two house-boys, Subri is incontestably the better. He is intelligent, quick, adaptable, and always gay. His general appearance of ferocity and the immense knife, carefully sharpened, which he keeps under his pillow at night, are mere irrelevancies! So is the fact that whenever he requests leave of absence it is to visit some relation who is incarcerated at Damascus or elsewhere for murder! The murders, Subri explains seriously, have all been *necessary*. It has been a matter of honor or family prestige. This is borne out, he says, by the fact that none of their sentences are long ones.

Subri, then, is by far the more desirable servant; but Mansur, by right of seniority of service, is the head boy. Mansur, though fulfilling Max's dictum that he is too stupid to be anything but honest, is nevertheless, to put it bluntly, a pain in the neck!

And Mansur, since he is the head boy, attends to the needs of Max and myself, whilst the Colonel and

Bumps, supposedly inferior in rank, have the services of the intelligent and merry Subri.

Sometimes, in the very early morning, a feeling of loathing comes over me for Mansur! He enters the room after knocking about six times, being in doubt as to whether the repeated "Come in" can really be meant for him. He stands inside, breathing laboriously, and holding, precariously balanced, two cups of strong tea.

Slowly, breathing stertorously, and shuffling his feet, he advances across the floor and puts down one cup on the chair beside my bed, slopping most of it into the saucer as he does so. With him comes a strong aroma, at best of onions, at worst of garlic. Neither of these is really appreciated at five A.M.

The spilling of the tea fills Mansur with despair. He stares down at the cup and saucer, shaking his head, and poking at it doubtfully with a finger and thumb.

In a ferocious half-awakened voice I say: "Leave it!"

Mansur starts, breathes hard, and shuffles across the room to Max, where he repeats the performance.

He then turns his attention to the washstand. He picks up the enamel basin, carries it cautiously to the door, and empties it outside. He returns with it, pours about an inch of water in, and goes over it laboriously with one finger. This process takes about ten minutes. He then sighs, goes out, returns with a kerosene tin of hot water, puts it down and slowly shuffles out, shutting the door in such a way that it immediately comes open again!

I then drink off the cold tea, rise, clean the basin myself, throw out the water, latch the door properly, and start the day.

After breakfast, Mansur addresses himself to the task of "doing the bedroom." His first procedure, after slopping a good deal of water about in the neighborhood of the washstand, is to dust very carefully and methodically. This is not bad as a performance, but it occupies an immense amount of time.

Satisfied with the first stage of housework, Mansur goes out, fetches a native broom, returns with it, and begins to sweep furiously. Having raised a terrific dust, so that the air is unbreathable, Mansur makes the beds —either in such a way that your feet are immediately exposed when you get in, or else by his second method, which involves half the length of the bedclothes being tucked under the mattress, the top half reaching only to one's waist. I pass over such minor idiosyncrasies as laying the sheets and blankets in alternate layers and putting both pillow-cases on one pillow. These flights of fancy only occur on clean linen days.

Finally nodding his head in approval, Mansur staggers out of the room, exhausted by nervous strain and hard work. He takes himself and his duties very seriously, and is intensely conscientious. This attitudue of his has made a deep impression on the rest of the staff, and Dimitri, the cook, says quite seriously to Max: "Subri is most willing and industrious, but he has not, of course, the *knowledge* and *experience* of Mansur, who is trained in all the ways of the Khwajas!" Not to subvert discipline, Max perforce makes sounds of agreement, but both he and I look yearningly at Subri as he cheerfully shakes and folds the Colonel's clothes.

I once officiously tried to instill into Mansur my own ideas of the routine of housework, but it was a mistaken move. I merely confused him and roused all his native obstinacy.

"The ideas of the Khatūn are not practical," he said sadly to Max. "She demands that I put tea leaves on the *floor*. But tea leaves are in a *teapot* for *drinking*. And how can I dust the rooms *after* sweeping? I take the dust from the tables and let it fall on the ground, and *then* I sweep it from the ground. That is only reasonable."

Mansur is very strong upon what is reasonable. A demand of the Colonel's for jam to add to his *leben* (sour milk) brought the immediate reproof from Mansur: "No, it is not necessary!"

Some vestiges of military tradition cling around Mansur. His answer to a summons is the immediate reply: *"Présent!"* And he announces lunch and dinner with the simple formula: *"La Soupe!"*

The time of day when Mansur is really in his element is the hour of the bath, just before dinner. Here Mansur presides, and does not have to do anything himself. Under his commanding eye, Ferhid and Ali bring large kerosene tins of boiling water and others of cold water (mostly mud) from the kitchen and set out the baths—which are large, round copper affairs, like immense preserving-pans. Later, still under Mansur's supervision, Ferhid and Ali stagger out with the copper pans and empty them, usually immediately outside the front door, so that if you go out unwarily after dinner you slide on liquid mud and fall headlong.

Ali, since his promotion to postboy and the acquisition of the bicycle, is getting a soul above menial chores. To the worried Ferhid is allotted the endless plucking of fowls and the ritualistic washing up of meals, which involves an immense quantity of soap and hardly any water.

On the rare occasions when I step into the kitchen to "show" Dimitri the preparation of some European dish, the highest standards of hygiene and general purity are at once insisted upon.

If I pick up a perfectly clean looking bowl, it is at once taken from me and handed to Ferhid.

"Ferhid, clean this for the Khatūn to use."

Ferhid seizes the bowl, smears the interior of it painstakingly with yellow soap, applies a brisk polish to the soapy surface, and returns it to me. I have an inner misgiving that a soufflé flavored heavily with soap will not really be nice, but stifle it, and force myself to proceed.

The whole thing is most shattering to the nerves. To begin with, the temperature of the kitchen is usually about 99° F., and to keep it even as cool as that there is only a tiny aperture to admit light, so that the whole effect is a sweltering gloom. Added to that is the disorganizing effect of the complete confidence and reverence expressed in every face surrounding me. There are a good many faces, for in addition to Dimitri, the slave Ferhid, and the haughty Ali, there have also come in to watch in the proceedings: Subri, Mansur, Serkis the carpenter, the waterman, and any odd workmen who may be doing a job on the house. The kitchen is small, the crowd is large. They close round me with admiring and reverent eyes, watching my every action. I begin to get nervous, and feel that everything is sure to go wrong. I drop an egg on the floor and break it. So complete is the confidence reposed in me that for quite a minute, everyone takes this to be part of the ritual!

I proceed, getting hotter and hotter and more and more unhinged. The pans are different from any I have ever known, the egg-whisk has an unexpectedly detachable handle, everything I use is a curious shape or size. . . . I pull myself together, and resolve desperately that, whatever the result may be, I shall pretend that it is what I have intended!

Actually the results fluctuate. Lemon curd is a great success; shortbread is so uneatable that we secretly bury it; a vanila soufflé, for a wonder, goes right; whereas Chicken Maryland (owing, as I realize later, to the extreme freshness and incredible age of the chicken) is so tough that one cannot get one's teeth through it!

I can say, however, that I know by now what to impart and what to leave well alone. No dish that needs to be eaten as soon as it is cooked should ever be attempted in the East. Omelettes, soufflés, chip potatoes, will inevitably be made a good hour beforehand and placed in the oven to mature, and no amount of remonstrance will avail. Anything, on the other hand, however elaborate, that requires long preparation beforehand and which can be kept waiting will turn out successfully. Soufflés and omelettes were regretfully erased from Dimitri's list. On the other hand, no chef could turn out regularly, day after day, a more perfect mayonnaise.

One other point may be mentioned in the culinary

line. This is the dish known familiarly to us as "biftek." Again and again the announcement of this delicacy arouses hopes in us, hopes doomed each time to disappointment when a platter containing some frizzled-up little bits of gristly meat is placed before us.

"It doesn't," the Colonel would say sadly, "even *taste* like beef."

And that, of course, is the real explanation—there never is any beef.

The butcher's shop is represented by a very simple proceeding. From time to time Michel departs with the lorry to a neighboring village or tribe. He returns, flings open the back of Mary, and out fall eight sheep!

These sheep are dispatched one at a time as needed, strict orders being given on my account that they should *not* be slaughtered exactly in front of the living-room windows! I also object to seeing Ferhid advancing upon the chickens, a long, sharp knife in hand.

This squeamishness of the Khatūn's is treated indulgently by the staff as another Western peculiarity.

Once, when we were digging near Mosul, our old foreman came to Max in great excitement.

"You must take your Khatūn to Mosul tomorrow. There is a great event. There is to be a *hanging*—a woman! Your Khatūn will enjoy it very much! She must on no account miss it!"

My indifference, and, indeed, repugnance, to this treat stupified him.

"But it is a *woman*," he insisted. "Very seldom do we have the hanging of a woman. It is a Kurdish woman who has poisoned three husbands! Surely—surely the Khatūn would not like to miss *that!*"

My firm refusal to attend lowered me in his eyes a good deal. He left us sadly, to enjoy the hanging by himself.

Even in other ways unexpected squeamishness overtakes one. Though indifferent to the fate of chickens and turkeys (unpleasant gobbling creatures), we once bought a nice fat goose. Unfortunately it turned out to be a companionable goose. It had clearly lived in its

village as one of the family. On the very first evening
it tried determinedly to share Max's bath. It was always pushing open a door and putting a beak in, in a
hopeful "I'm lonely" fashion. As the days passed we
got desperate. Nobody could bring themselves to order
the goose to be killed.

Eventually the cook took it upon himself. The goose
was duly served up, richly stuffed in native fashion,
and certainly looking and smelling delicious. Alas, none
of us enjoyed a morsel! It was the most depressed meal
we ever ate.

Bumps disgraces himself here one day when Dimitri
serves up proudly a lamb—head, paws, and all. Bumps
takes one look at it and rushes headlong from the room.

But to return to the problem of "biftek." After a
sheep has been slaughtered and dismembered it is
served in the following order: The shoulder, or some
such portion, stuffed with spices and rice and all sewn
up (Dimitri's grand dish); then the legs; then a platter
of what used to be called in the last war "edible offal";
then a kind of stew with rice; and finally, the last re-
jected inglorious portions of the sheep, unworthy of
inclusion in the better dishes, determinedly fried for a
long period until well reduced in size and completely
leathery in consistency—the dish known as "biftek"!

Work on the mound has been proceeding satisfac-
torily—the entire lower half has turned out to be prehistoric. We have been digging on one portion of the
mound a "deep cut" from the top to virgin soil. This
has given us fifteen layers of successive occupations.
Of these the lower ten are prehistoric. After 1500 B. C.
the mound was abandoned, presumably because denudation had set in and the levels were no longer good.
There are, as always, some Roman and Islamic graves
which are purely intrusive. We always call them Roman
to the men to spare any Moslem susceptibilities, but
the men themselves are an irreverent lot. "It is *your*
grandfather we are digging up, Abdul!" "No, it is yours,
Daoud!" They laugh and joke freely.

We have found many interesting carved animal amulets, all of a fairly well-known type, but now suddenly some very curious figures begin to be produced. A small blackened bear, a lion's head, and, finally, a queer primitive human figure. Max has had his suspicions of them, but the human figure is too much. We have got a forger at work.

"And he's quite a clever fellow, too," says Max, turning the bear round appreciatively. "Nice bit of work."

Detective work proceeds. The objects turn up in one corner of the dig and are usually found by one or other of two brothers. These men come from a village about ten kilometers away. One day, in quite another part of the dig, a suspicious-looking bitumen "spoon" turns up. It has been "found" by a man from the same village. Bakshish is given as usual and nothing is said.

But on pay-day comes the big exposure! Max displays the exhibits, makes an impassioned speech of condemnation, denounces them as trickery, and publicly destroys them (though he has kept the bear as a curiosity). The men who have produced them are sacked, and depart quite cheerfully, though loudly proclaiming their innocence.

The next day the men are chuckling on the dig.

"The Khwaja knows," they say. "He is very learned in antiquities. You cannot deceive his eyes."

Max is sad, because he would like very much to know exactly how the forgeries were made. Their excellent workmanship arouses his approbation.

One can make to oneself now a picture of Chagar as it must have been five to three thousand years ago. In the prehistoric times it must have been on a much-frequented caravan route, connecting Harran and Tell Halaf and on through the Jebel Sinjar into Iraq and the Tigris, and so to ancient Nineveh. It was one of a network of great trading centers.

Sometimes one feels a personal touch—a potter who has set his mark on the base of his pot, a *cache* in a wall where there is a small pot full of gold earrings, the dowry, perhaps, of the daughter of the house. Then a personal touch nearer our own times—a metal counter, with the name Hans Krauwinkel of Nuremberg, struck in about A.D. 1600, and which lay in an Islamic grave, showing that there was contact between this obscure region and Europe at that time.

In the age roughly perhaps five thousand years ago, there are some very lovely incised pots—to my mind real things of beauty—all made by hand.

There are the Madonnas of that age, too—turbanned figures with big breasts, grotesque and primitive, yet representing, no doubt, help and consolation.

There is also the fascinating development of the "bukranium" *motif* on pottery, starting as a simple ox's head, and becoming less naturalistic and more formal until it has gone so far that you would not recognize it at all if you did not know of the intervening steps. (In fact it is, I realize with dismay, exactly the simple pattern of a printed silk frock I sometimes wear! Oh, well, "bukranium" has a good deal pleasanter sound than a "running lozenge"!)

The day has come when the first spade is to be put into Tell Brak. It is quite a solemn moment.

By the combined efforts of Serkis and Ali one or two rooms are in order. The waterman, the grand horse which is not an old woman, the cart, the barrels—all is in readiness.

The Colonel and Bumps depart to Brak the night before to sleep there and be up on the mound at early dawn.

Max and I arrive there about eight o'clock. The Colonel, alas, has spent a sadly disturbed night wrestling with bats! It sems that the tower-room is literally infested with bats—creatures which the Colonel holds in great aversion.

Bumps reports that every time he awoke during the night the Colonel was barging about the room, lunging wildly at bats with a bath-towel.

We stayed a little while watching the proceedings on the dig.

The gloomy waterman came up to me and poured out a long tale of what seemed to be bitter woe. When Max came up, I asked him to find out what it was all about.

It appeared that the waterman has a wife and ten children somewhere near Jerablus, and that his heart is distracted by absence from them. Could he have an advance of money and send for them to join him?

I plead for a favorable reply. Max is a little dubious. A woman in the house, he says, will lead to trouble.

On our way back to Chagar we meet large quantities of our workmen walking across country to the new dig.

"El hamdu lillah!" they cry. "Will there be work for us tomorrow?"

"Yes, there will be work."

They praise God again and tramp on.

We spend two uneventful days at home, and now it is our turn to do a session at Brak. Nothing of great moment has turned up there yet, but it promises well, and the houses, etc., are of the right period.

A strong wind is blowing to-day from the south—the most detestable of winds. It makes you irritable and nervy. We set out, prepared for the worst, with gum-boots, mackintoshes, and even umbrellas. Serki's assurances that he has mended the roof we do not take too seriously. Tonight will be, as Michel would say, a case of *Sawi Proba*.

The route to Brak is all across country with no track. We are halfway there when we overtake two workmen of ours trudging towards "the work." Since we have room, Max stops Mary and offers them a lift, which causes great jubilation. Walking at their heels, with a small bit of frayed rope round its neck, is a dog.

The men get in and Michel prepares to drive off. Max asks what about the dog? We will take their dog too. It is *not* their dog, they say. It just appeared suddenly out of the desert.

We look more closely at the dog. Though of no known breed, it is clearly a European mixture! In shape it resembles a Skye terrier, with Dandy Dinmont coloring, and a definite touch of Cairn. It is immensely long, has brilliant amber eyes, and a rather common pale-brown nose. It looks neither wretched nor sorry for itself nor timorous—most unlike the average dog of the East. Sitting down comfortably, it surveys us cheerfully, with a slight wag of the tail.

Max says we will take it along with us, and orders Michel to pick it up and put it in.

Michel flinches. "It will bite me," he says dubiously.

"Yes, yes," say the two Arabs. "Assuredly it will have your meat! Better leave it here, Khwaja."

"Pick it up and put it in, you damned fool!" says Max to Michel.

Michel nerves himself and advances on the dog, which turns its head pleasantly towards him.

Michel retreats rapidly. I lose patience, jump out, pick up the dog, and get back into Mary with it. Its ribs are sticking through the skin. We drive on to Brak, where the newcomer is handed over to Ferhid, with instructions that a large meal is to be given to her. We also debate a name, and decide on Miss Ostapenko (since I am just reading *Tobit Transplanted*). Owing mainly to Bumps, however, Miss Ostapenko is never known as anything else but Hiyou. Hiyou turns out to be a dog of amazing character. Avid for life, she is absolutely intrepid, and shows no fear of anything or any one. She is perfectly good-humored and good-tempered, and absolutely determined at all times to do exactly as she likes. She obviously possesses the nine lives usually attributed to cats. If she is shut in, she manages somehow to get out. If shut out, she manages to get in—once by eating a two-foot hole in a mud-brick wall. She attends all meals, and is so insistent that you cannot withstand her. She does not beg—but demands.

I feel convinced that someone took Hiyou out with a stone attached to her neck by a rope and tried to drown her, but that Hiyou, determined to enjoy life, bit through the rope, swam ashore, and started cheerfully across the desert, picking up the two men by her infallible instinct. In confirmation of my theory, Hiyou will come with us when summoned everywhere except down to the Jaghjagha. There she stands firm across the path, more or less shakes her head, and returns to the house. "No, thank you," she says, "I don't like being drowned! Tedious!"

The Colonel, we are glad to hear, has passed a better night. Serkis has ejected most of the bats in repairing the roof, and in addition the Colonel has rigged up a rather Heath Robinsonian device, involving a large bowl of water, into which the bats eventually fall and are drowned. The mechanism, as explained to us by the Colonel, is very complicated, and the preparation of it somewhat cut short his hours of sleep.

We go up to the mound and have lunch in a spot sheltered from the wind. Even then a large proportion of sand and dust is absorbed with every bite. Everybody is looking cheerful, and even the melancholy waterman displays a certain pride as he drives to and from the Jaghjagha, bringing up the men's water. He drives it to the foot of the mound, and there donkeys take it up in water-jars. The whole thing has a Biblical aspect that is rather fascinating.

When Fidos comes, we exchange farewells, the Colonel and Bumps depart in Mary for Chagar, and we take our two days' duty at Brak.

The tower-room looks quite attractive. There is matting on the floor and a couple of rugs. We have a jug and basin, a table, two chairs, two camp-beds, towels, sheets, blankets, and even books. The windows have been insecurely fastened up, and we retire to bed after a rather peculiar meal, served gloomily by Ferhid and cooked by Ali. It is mainly very liquid spinach, with minute islands in it, which we suspect are once again "Biftek!"

We pass a good night. Only one bat materializes, and Max lures it out with a torch. We decide to tell the Colonel that his stories of hundreds of bats are a gross exaggeration and probably due to drink. At four-fifteen Max is called with tea and starts for the mound. I go to sleep again. At six tea is brought in for me. Max returns for breakfast at eight. The meal is served, with a flourish—boiled eggs, tea, Arab bread, two pots of jam, and a tin of custard powder (!). A few minutes later a second course is brought in—scrambled eggs.

Max murmurs: *"Trop de zèle,"* and fearing the imminent arrival of an omelette, sends word to the invisible Ali that what we have had will do nicely. Ferhid sighs and departs with the message. He returns, his forehead corrugated with perplexity and anxiety. We fear a major catastrophe—but no, he merely asks: "Will you require oranges sent up with your luncheon?"

Bumps and the Colonel come over at midday. Bumps has a good deal of trouble with his topee owing to the howling wind. Michel arrives helpfully to apply *Forca,* but remembering last time, Bumps avoids him with dexterity.

Our normal lunch is cold meat and salad, but Ali's ambitious soul has soared to better things, and we eat slices of fried aubergine, tepid and only half-cooked, greasy cold fried potatoes, little discs of "biftek" fried very hard, and a dish of salad complete with dressing applied to it many hours ago, so that the whole thing is an orgy of cold green grease!

Max says he will be sorry to damp Ali's well-meaning efforts, but he will have to curb his imagination.

We find Abd es Salaam employing the lunch-hour by treating the men to a long, moral harangue of a really nauseating character.

"See how fortunate you are!" he shouts, waving his arms. "Is not all done for you? Is not all thought taken for you? You are permitted to bring your food here,

to eat it in the courtyard of the house! Immense wages
are paid you—yes, whether you find anything or nothing, that money is paid to you! What generosity, what
nobility! *And* that is not all! In addition to these big
wages, further money is paid to you for everything that
you find! Like a father the Khwaja watches over you;
he keeps you even from doing each other bodily harm!
If you are ill with fever, he gives you medicine! If
your bowels are shut, he gives you opening medicine
of first-class power! How happy, how fortunate is your
lot! And yet further generosity! Does he leave you to
work thirsty? Does he make you provide your own
water to drink? No! No, indeed! Though under no
obligation, freely, in his great generosity, he *brings*
water for you to the mound, all the way from the Jaghjagha! Water brought at vast expense in a cart drawn
by a *horse!* Think of the expense, of the outlay! What
wonderful good fortune is yours to be employed by
such a man!"

We steal away, and Max remarks thoughtfully that
he wonders some of the workmen don't murder Abd
es Salaam. *He* would, he says, if he were one. Bumps
says that, on the contrary, the workmen are just lap-
ping it up. It is true. Nods and grunts of appreciation
are heard, one man turns to another.

"It is reasonable what he says. Water is brought for
us. Yes, there is indeed generosity here. He is right.
We are fortunate. He is a wise man, this Abd es
Salaam."

Bumps says it beats him how they stick it. But I
disagree. I remember with what avidity one lapped up
really moral tales as a child! The Arab has something
of that direct *naif* approach to life. The sententious
Abd es Salaam is preferred to the more modern and
less sanctimonious Alawi. Moreover, Abd es Salaam
is a great dancer, and in the evenings in the courtyard
of the Brak house the men, led by old Abd es Salaam,
dance long, intricate measures—or what is really more
a *pattern*—sometimes until far into the night. How
they can do it and be up on the mound again at five

A.M. is a mystery. But then there is the mystery of how men from villages three, five, and ten kilometers away can arrive exact to the minute at sunrise every day! They have no clocks or watches, and they must start at times varying from twenty minutes to over an hour before sunrise, but there they are. They are neither late nor early. Surprising to see them, too, at Fidos when work is over (half an hour before sunset), throw up their baskets, laugh, shoulder their picks, and *run*— yes, *run* gaily off on the ten-kilometer distance home again! Their only break has been half an hour for breakfast and an hour for lunch, and according to our standards they have always been undernourished. It is true that they work in what may be called leisurely fashion, with only occasional spurts of frenzied digging or running when a wave of gaiety sweeps over them, but it is all really hard manual labor. The pickman, perhaps, has the best of it, for when he has loosened the surface of his area he sits down to enjoy a cigarette whilst the spademan fills the baskets. The basket-boys get no repose except what they snatch for themselves. But they are quite adroit at doing that, moving in slow motion to the dump, or taking a long while to search their baskets through.

On the whole they are a wonderfully healthy lot. There is a good deal of eye soreness, and they are much preoccupied with constipation! There is, I believe, a good deal of tuberculosis nowadays, which has been brought to them by Western civilization. But their recuperative powers are marvelous. One man will cut open another's head, leaving a horrible-looking wound. The man will ask us to treat it and bind it up, but looks amazed at a suggestion that he should knock off work and go home. "What, for *this!* It is hardly a headache!" And within two or three days the whole place is healed up, in spite of the definitely unhygienic treatment which the man himself has doubtless applied to it as soon as he gets home.

One man who had a large and painful boil on

his leg was sent home by Max, since he obviously had fever.

"You shall be paid just the same as if you were here."

The man grunted and went off. But that afternoon Max suddenly caught sight of him working. "What are you doing here? I sent you home."

"I went home, Khwaja (eight kilometers). But when I got home it was dull. No conversation! Only the women. So I walked back. And see, it has been *good,* the swelling has broken!"

Today we return to Chagar and the other two come to Brak. It feels great luxury to get back to our own house. On arrival we find that the Colonel has been busy pasting up notices everywhere, mostly of an insulting character! He has also tidied with such zest that we are quite unable to find anything we need. We meditate reprisals! Finally we cut out pictures of Mrs. Simpson from some old papers and pin them up in the Colonel's room!

There are a lot of photographs to be taken and developed, and, as it is a hot day, I emerge from my darkroom feeling exactly like a bit of wall fungus myself. The staff is kept busy supplying me with comparatively pure water. The grosser mud is first strained off, and it is finally strained through cotton wool into various buckets. By the time it is actually used for the negatives, only stray sand and dust from the air have got in, and the results are quite satisfactory. One of our workmen comes up to Max and asks for five days' leave of absence.

"Why?"

"I have to go to gaol!"

Today has been memorable for a rescue. There was rain in the night, and this morning the ground was still soggy. About twelve o'clock a wild-looking horseman arrived, riding with the wildness and desperation of one who brings the good news from Aix

to Ghent, etc. Actually he brings bad news. The Colonel
and Bumps have set out to come to us and are bogged
halfway. The horseman is sent back at once with two
spades, and we fit out a rescue party in Poilu. Five
men go with Serkis in charge. They take spades and
extra boards and depart very gaily, singing!

Max yells after them not to get bogged themselves.
Actually this is exactly what happens, but, fortunately,
only a few hundred yards from where Mary is in distress. Her back-axle is buried in mud and her crew
are very weary, having been trying to dig her out for
five solid hours, and having been exasperated almost
to madness by Michel's well-meant exhortations and
commands, all uttered in his usual high, whining fal-
setto, and consisting mainly of *"Forca!"* as he breaks
the third jack in succession! With the assistance of the
toughs (selected for their heftiness), and under the
more able direction of Serkis, Mary consents to come
out of the mud, which she does very suddenly, coating
everybody from head to foot and leaving a yawning
hole behind her, christened by the Colonel "Mary's
Grave."

There has been a good deal of rain falling during
our latest spell at Brak, and Serkis' roof has not quite
stood up to the strain. Moreover, the window boards
swing open, and gusts of wind and rain sweep through
the room. Fortunately the worst rain falls on our "day
off," so that the work is not held up, though our pro-
jected excursion to the Kawkab volcano is.

Incidentally, we nearly have a riot over this, as the
ten-day period ends on Saturday, and Abd es Salaam,
told to announce to the men that there would be no
work the next day, like the complete old bungler he
is, bleats out: "Tomorrow is Sunday—*therefore,* no
work!"

Immediately there is an uproar! What! Are all the
good Moslem gentlemen to be insulted and sacrificed
to a miserable twenty Armenian Christians? A fiery
gentleman called Abbas 'Id tries to organize a strike.
Max then makes an oration, stating that if he wants

a holiday on Sunday, Monday, Tuesday, Wednesday, Friday, or Saturday, a holiday there will be. As for Abbas 'Id, he is never to show his face on the mound again! The Armenians, who are courting assassination by chuckling in triumph, are told to hold their tongues, after which pay-day begins. Max ensconces himself in Mary, Michel staggers out of the house with sacks of money (no longer mejidis, thank heaven!—they have been made illegal, and Syrian currency is now *de rigueur*), which he disposes in the lorry. Max's face appears at the window of the driving-seat (looking rather like a booking-clerk at a railway station), Michel takes a chair into the lorry and assumes control of the cash, forming the coins up in piles, and sighing deeply as he contemplates how much money is going into Moslem hands!

Max opens an immense ledger and the fun starts. Gang after gang parade as their names are called, and come up and draw what is owing to them. Terrific feats of arithmetic have been performed well into the small hours the night before, as the daily bakshish of each man is checked up and added to his wages.

The inequality of Fate is very marked on pay-day. Some men draw a heavy bonus, some hardly anything. There are a lot of jokes and quips, and everyone, even those passed over by Fortune, are very gay. A tall, handsome Kurdish woman rushes up to her husband, who is counting over what he has received.

"What have you got? Show it to me?" Without scruple she seizes the whole amount and goes off with it.

Two refined-looking Arabs turn their faces gently aside, shocked by such a spectacle of unwomanly (and unmanly) behavior!

The Kurdish woman reappears from her mud-hut and screams abuse at her husband for the way he is untethering a donkey. The Kurd, a big handsome man, sighs sadly. Who would be a Kurdish husband?

There is a saying that if an Arab robs you in the desert, he will beat you but leave you to live, but if a Kurd robs you he will kill you just for the pleasure of it!

Perhaps being henpecked at home stimulates fierceness abroad!

At last, after two hours, everyone is paid. A little misunderstanding between Daoud Suleiman and Daoud Suleiman Mohammed has been adjusted, to everyone's satisfaction. Abdullah has returned smiling, to explain that ten francs fifty has been allotted to him in error. Little Mahmoud expostulates shrilly over forty-five centimes—"two beads, a rim of pottery, and a bit of obsidian, Khwaja, and the day was last Thursday!" All claims, counterclaims, etc., have been examined and adjusted. Information is sought as to who continues work and who is going to leave. Nearly everybody leaves. "But after the next period—who knows, Khwaja?"

"Yes," says Max, "when your money is spent!"

"As you say, Khwaja."

Friendly greetings and farewells are said. That night there is singing and dancing in the courtyard.

Back at Chagar and a lovely hot day. The Colonel has been spluttering with rage over the behavior of Poilu, who has let him down every single day at Brak lately. On each occasion Ferhid has arrived, given assurances that the car is quite all right, nothing wrong with it, and on his demonstration of this fact it immediately starts. The Colonel feels this an additional insult.

Michel comes up and explains in his high voice that all that is needed is to clear the carburetor—it is very simple, he will show the Colonel. Michel then proceeds to do his favorite trick of sucking petrol up into his mouth, gargling freely with it, and finally drinking it. The Colonel looks on with a face of cold disgust. Michel nods his head, smiles happily, says persuasively to the Colonel: "Sawi Proba?" and proceeds to light a cigarette. We hold our breath, waiting to see Michel's throat go up in flames, but nothing happens.

Various minor complications occur. Four men are

sacked for persistent fighting. Alawi and Yahya have a quarrel and will not speak to each other. One of our house-rugs has been stolen. The Sheikh is very indignant, and is holding a court of inquiry into the matter. This we have the pleasure of observing from afar—a circle of white-clad, bearded men are sitting out in the plain with their heads together. "They hold it there," explains Mansur, "so that none can overhear the secret things they say."

The subsequent proceedings are very Eastern. The Sheikh comes to us, assures us that the malefactors are now known to him, that all shall be dealt with, and our rug restored.

What actually happens is, that the Sheikh beats up six of his particular enemies and possibly blackmails a few more. The rug does not materialize, but the Sheikh is in high good humor and seems quite flush of cash again.

Abd es Salaam comes secretively to Max. "*I* will tell you who stole your rug. It is the Sheikh's brother-in-law, the Yezidi Sheikh. He is a very evil man, but his sister is handsome."

Hope of a little pleasant persecution of Yezidis shows in Abd es Salaam's eye, but Max declares that the rug is to be written off as a loss and no more done about it. "In future," says Max, looking severely at Mansur and Subri, "better care is to be taken, and the rugs are not to be left to lie about in the sun outside."

The next sad incident is that the Customs men arrive and pinch two of our workmen for smoking smuggled Iraqi cigarettes. This is very bad luck on the particular two, as in actual fact two hundred and eighty men (our present pay-roll) are all smoking smuggled Iraqi cigarettes! The Customs official seeks an interview with Max. "This is a serious offense," he says. "Out of courtesy to you, Khwaja, we have refrained from arresting these men on your dig. It might not be to your honor."

"I thank you for your kindness and delicacy," Max replies.

"We suggest, however, that *you* should sack them without pay, Khwaja."

"That may hardly be. It is not for *me* to enforce the laws of this country. I am a foreigner. These men have contracted to work for me and I have contracted to pay them. I cannot withhold pay due to them."

The matter is settled at last (with the assent of the guilty parties) by two fines being stopped out of the men's pay and handed to the Customs officer.

"Inshallah!" say the men, shrugging their shoulders, as they return to work. The soft-hearted Max is a little over-generous with the bakshish that week to the two culprits, and pay-day finds them cheerful. They do not suspect Max of beneficence, but ascribe their good fortune to the infinite compassion of Allah.

We have made another excursion to Kamichlie. By now it has all the excitement of a visit to Paris or London. The procedure has been much the same— Harrods, desultory conversation with M. Yannakos, lengthy sessions in the Bank, but enlivened this time by the presence of a supreme dignitary of the Maronite Church, complete with jewelled cross, luxuriant hair, and robes of purple. Max nudges me to offer "Monseigneur" my chair, which I do reluctantly, and feeling rather fiercely Protestant. (Note.—Would I, in similar circumstances, offer the only chair to the Archbishop of York if I happened to be sitting in it? I decide that if I did, he wouldn't take it!) The Archimandrite, or the Grand Mufti or whatever he is, does, sinking down with a sigh of satisfaction and giving me a benignant glance.

Michel, it need hardly be said, tries our tempers to the utmost! He makes ridiculous purchases of a highly economical order. He also goes with Mansur to see about the purchase of a second horse, and Mansur, fired with equine passion, rides the said horse right into the local barber's shop, where Max is having his hair cut!

"Get out, you fool!" yells Max.

"It is a fine horse," shouts Mansur, "and quiet!"

At this moment the horse rears up, and, threatened by two immense front hoofs, everyone in the barber's shop ducks for cover.

Mansur and the horse are ejected, Max returns to finish his haircut, and postpones all that he wishes to say to Mansur until later.

We have a very delicious and recherché lunch with the French Commandant at the Barracks, invite some of the French officers to come out and see us, and return to Harrods to see what Michel's latest enormities are. It is looking like rain, so we decide to start back at once.

The horse has been purchased, and Mansur pleads that he may be allowed to ride it home.

Max says, if so he'll never get home.

I say it is an excellent idea, and please do let Mansur ride the horse home.

"You'll be so stiff you won't be able to move," says Max.

Mansur says he is never stiff when riding a horse.

It is arranged that Mansur is to return on the horse the following day. The mail is a day late, so he will be able to bring that with him.

Rain falls as we drive back (accompanied by the usual uncomfortable hens and derelict humans). We have fantastic skids, but we just get home before the track becomes impassable.

The Colonel has just got back from Brak and has had a lot more trouble with bats. Luring them with an electric torch to the basin has been very successful, only, as he has spent all night doing this, he hasn't had much sleep. We say coldly that *we* never see any bats!

Among our workmen is one who is able to read and write! His name is Yusuf Hassan, and he is quite one of the laziest men on the dig. I never once arrive on the mound to find Yusuf actually working. He has always just finished digging his patch, or is about to begin, or has paused to light a cigarette. He is somewhat proud of his literacy, and one day amuses himself and his friends by writing on an empty cigarette packet: "Saleh Birro has been drowned in the Jaghjagha." Everybody is much amused by this piece of erudition and wit!

The empty packet gets caught up with an empty bread-bag, is crammed into a flour sack, and in due course the sack gets returned to its place of origin—the village of Hanzir. Here somebody notices the inscription. It is taken to a learned man; he reads it. Forthwith the news is sent on to the village of Germayir, Saleh Birro's home-town. Result: On the following Wednesday a great cavalcade of mourners—men, weeping women, wailing children arrive at Tell Brak.

"Alas, alas!" they cry, "Saleh Birro, our loved one, has been drowned in the Jaghjagha! We come for his body!"

The first thing they then see is Saleh Birro himself, happily digging and spitting in his appointed pit of earth. Stupefaction, explanations, and forthwith Saleh Birro, mad with rage, attempts to brain Yusuf Hassan with his pick. A friend on each side joins in, the Colonel comes up and orders them to stop (vain hope!), and tries to find out what it is all about.

Court of inquiry then held by Max and sentence pronounced.

Saleh Birro is sacked for one day—(a) for fighting, (b) for not stopping fighting when told. Yusuf Hassan is commanded to walk to Germayir (forty kilometres), and there explain and apologize for his singularly ill-omened idea. Also to be fined two days' pay.

And the real moral is—Max points out afterwards to his own select circle—what very dangerous things reading and writing are!

Mansur, having been marooned for three days owing to the weather in Kamichlie, suddenly arrives more dead than alive on the horse. Not only is he unable to stand, but he has had the added woe of having purchased a large and delectable fish in Kamichlie, and in the enforced wait it has gone bad on him. For some unappreciated reason he has brought it with him! It is hastily buried, and Mansur retires, groaning to his bed, and is not seen for three days. We meanwhile enjoy the intelligent ministrations of Subri a good deal.

At last the expedition to the Kawkab takes place. Ferhid, his air of concentration greater than ever, volunteers to act as our guide, since he "knows the country." We cross the Jaghjagha by a rather precarious-looking bridge, and abandon ourselves to Ferhid's sad leadership.

Apart from the fact that Ferhid nearly dies of anxiety on the way, we do not do too badly. The Kawkab is always in sight, which is helpful, but the stony ground we have to cross is quite appalling, especially as we draw nearer to the extinct volcano.

Matters in the household were very strained before starting, a passionate quarrel about a small cake of soap having inflamed the whole staff. The foremen says coldly that they prefer not to come on the expedition, but the Colonel forces them to do so. They get into Mary from opposite sides and sit with their backs to each other! Serkis squats down like a hen in the back, and will speak to no one. Exactly who has quarrelled with who it is difficult to find out. However, by the time the ascension of the Kawkab is over all is forgotten. We were expecting a gentle sloping walk up to the top over ground carpeted with flowers, but, when we actually reach the place, the ascent is like the side of a house, and the ground is all slippery black cinders. Michel and Ferhid refuse firmly even to start, but the rest of us make the attempt. I give up soon, and settle down to enjoy the spectacle of the others slipping and panting and scrambling. Abd es Salaam goes up mostly on all fours!

There is a smaller crater, and on the lip of this we have lunch. There are flowers here in quantity, and it is a lovely moment. A marvelous view all round, with the

hills of the Jebel Sinjar not far away. The utter peace
is wonderful. A great wave of happiness surges over me,
and I realize how much I love this country, and how
complete and satisfying this life is. . . .

IX

ARRIVAL OF MAC

THE SEASON IS drawing to a close. The time has come for Mac to join us, and we are looking forward to seeing him. Bumps asks many questions about Mac, and displays incredulity at some of my statements. An extra pillow is needed, and we buy one in Kamichlie, the best we can find, but it is indubitably as hard as lead.

"The poor fellow can't sleep on *that*," says Bumps.

I assure him that Mac won't mind what he sleeps on.

"Fleas and bugs don't bite him; he never seems to have any luggage or any personal possessions shed about." I add reminiscently: "Just his plaid rug and his diary."

Bumps looks more incredulous than ever.

The day of Mac's arrival comes. It coincides with our day off and we plan a complicated expedition. The Colonel starts for Kamichlie at five-thirty A.M. in Poilu, and will combine meeting Mac with getting his hair cut. (This has to be done very often, as the Colonel insists on a closely military cut!)

We breakfast at seven and start at eight for Amuda, where we are to *rendezvous* with the others, and all go on to Ras-el-Ain, the idea being to examine a few mounds in that vicinity. (Our holidays are always busmen's holidays!) Subri and the gentle Dimitri also come on this expedition. They are exquisitely dressed, with shining boots and Homburg hats, and are wearing purple suits much too tight for them. Michel, warned by bitter experience, is wearing his working clothes, but he has put on white spats to mark his sense of holiday.

Amuda is as foul as ever, with even more carcasses of decaying sheep displayed than I remember before. Mac and the Colonel have not yet turned up, and I hazard the opinion that Poilu has, as usual, let the Colonel down.

However, they soon arrive, and after greetings and a few purchases (mainly bread; the Amuda bread is very good) we prepare to start, only to find that Poilu has lapsed from his good behavior and has got a flat tire. Michel and Subri attend quickly to this, whilst a crowd gathers round, pressing in closer and closer— always a habit of the Amudaites.

We get under way at last, but after about an hour Poilu repeats his bad behavior, and yet another tire goes. More repairs, and it now appears that none of Poilu's toilet apparatus is any good. His jack is defective and his pump a complete fiasco. Subri and Michel perform miracles by holding on to portions of tubing with their teeth and nails.

Having now lost an hour of valuable time we set off again. We next come to a wadi which is unexpectedly full of water—unusual so early in the season. We halt, and a discussion ensues as to whether we can rush it and get through.

Michel, Subri, and Dimitri are of the opinion that of course we can, if God is willing and merciful. Taking into consideration that if the Almighty is unwilling and disinclined to raise the chassis of Poilu by a miracle, we shall be stuck and probably not get out, we regretfully decide for discretion.

The local village is so much disappointed by our decision that we suspect that they derive a livelihood from pulling out submerged cars. Michel wades in to test the depth of the water, and we are all fascinated by the revelation of his underclothing! Strange white cotton garments tied with tapes round the ankles make their appearance—something like a Victorian Miss's pantalets!

We decide to lunch here by the wadi. After lunch, Max and I paddle our feet in it—delicious, till a snake suddenly darts out and quite puts us off paddling.

An old man comes and sits down beside us. There is the usual long silence after greetings have been given.

Then he inquires courteously if we are French? German? English?

English!

He nods his head. "Is it the English this country belongs to now? I cannot remember. I know it is no longer the Turks."

"No," we say; "the Turks have not been here since the war."

"A war?" says the old man, puzzled.

"The war that was fought twenty years ago."

He reflects. "I do not remember a war . . . Ah yes, about the time you mention, many 'asker went to and fro over the railway. That, then, was the war? We did not realize it was a war. It did not touch us here."

Presently, after another long silence, he rises, bids us farewell politely, and is gone.

We return by way of Tell Baindar, where what seems like thousands of black tents are pitched. It is the Beduin coming south for pasturage as the spring advances. There is water in the Wadi Wajh, and the whole scene is vibrant with life. In another two weeks, probably, it will be empty and silent once more.

I pick up one find on the slopes of Tell Baindar. It appears to be a small shell, but on examining it I see that it is actually made of clay and has traces of paint on it. It intrigues me, and I speculate vainly on who made it and why. Did it adorn a building, or a cosmetic box, or a dish? It is a *sea* shell. Who thought or knew of the sea here so far inland all those thousands of years ago? What pride of imagination and craftsmanship went to the making of it? I invite Max to speculate with me, but he says cautiously we have not got any data; but adds obligingly that he will look up parallels for me and see if the same type of thing has been found elsewhere. I do not even expect Mac to speculate—it is not in his constitution, and he is quite uninterested. Bumps is much more obliging, and consents willingly to play games with me on the subject. "Variations on the find of a pottery shell" continue for some time, but we end by uniting all together to fall upon the Colonel, who has gone all Roman on us (terrible solecism on a dig such as ours). I relent sufficiently to agree to take special trouble to photograph a Roman fibula brooch which has been among our (despised) finds, and even to allot it a plate all to itself!

We all arrive home in merry spirits and the Sheikh rushes out to greet Mac. "Ha, the Khwaja engineer!" He embraces him warmly on both cheeks.

Many chuckles from the Colonel, and Max warns him:

"Next year *you'll* be treated that way."

"Allow myself to be kissed by that disgusting old man?"

We all lay bets on the subject, the Colonel remaining very stiff and dignified. Max, he informs us, was greeted as Brother, and submitted to a very hearty embrace; "but it is not going to happen to *me*," says the Colonel firmly.

Rapturous greeting of Mac by the foremen. They pour out Arabic, and Mac, as usual, responds in English.

"Ah, the Khwaja Mac!" sighs Alawi. "Still will it be necessary for him to whistle for all he wants!"

An immense dinner materializes in next to no time,

and after it, tired and comfortable, with special delicacies in honor of holiday and Mac's arrival (Turkish Delight, preserved aubergines, bars of chocolate and cigars), we sit and talk, for once, of subjects other than archaeology.

We come to the question of religions generally—a very vexed question in this particular part of the world, for Syria is full of fiercely fanatical sects of all kinds, all willing to cut each other's throats for the good cause! From there we fall to discussing the story of the Good Samaritan. All the Bible and New Testament stories take on a particular reality and interest out here. They are couched in the language and ideology which we hear daily all around us, and I am often struck by the way the emphasis sometimes shifts from what one has commonly accepted. As a small instance, it come to me quite suddenly that in the story of Jezebel, it is the painting of her face and the tiring of her hair that emphasizes in puritanical Protestant surroundings what exactly a "Jezebel" stands for. But out here it is not the painting and tiring—for all virtuous women paint their faces (or tattoo them), and apply henna to their hair—it is the fact that Jezebel *looked out of the window*—a definitely immodest action!

The New Testament comes very near when I ask Max to repeat to me the gist of long conversations that he has with the Sheikh, for their exchanges consist almost entirely of parables—to illustrate your wishes or your demands, you tell a story with a point to it, the other counters with another story which turns the tables, and so on. Nothing is ever couched in direct language.

The Good Samaritan story has a reality here which it cannot have in an atmosphere of crowded streets, police, ambulances, hospitals, and public assistance. If a man fell by the wayside on the broad desert track from Hasetshe to Der-ez-Zor, the story could easily happen today, and it illustrates the enormous virtue compassion has in the eyes of all desert folk.

How many of us, Max asks suddenly, would really

succor another human being in conditions where there were no witnesses, no force of public opinion, no knowledge or censure of a failure to extend aid?

"Everyone, of course," says the Colonel firmly.

"No, but would they?" persists Max. "A man is lying dying. Death, remember, is not very important here. You are in a hurry. You have business to do. You do not want delay or bother. The man is nothing whatever to you. And nobody will ever know if you just hurry on, saying that, after all, it isn't your business, and somebody else will come along presently," etc., etc.

We all sit back and think, and we are all, I think, a little shattered. . . . Are we so sure, after all, of our essential humanity?

After a long pause Bumps says slowly: "I *think* I would. . . . Yes, I think I would. I might go on, and then, perhaps, feel ashamed and come back."

The Colonel agrees.

"Just so; one wouldn't feel *comfortable*."

Max says he thinks *he* would, too, but he isn't nearly so sure about himself as he would like to be, and I concur with him.

We all sit silent for a while, and then I realize that, as usual, Mac has made no contribution.

"What would you do, Mac?"

Mac starts slightly, coming out of a pleasant abstraction.

"Me?" His tone is slightly surprised. "Oh, I would go on. I wouldn't stop."

"You wouldn't? Definitely?"

We all look interestedly at Mac, who shakes his gentle head.

"People die so much out here. One feels that a little sooner or later doesn't matter. I really wouldn't expect any one to stop for *me*."

No, that is true, Mac wouldn't.

His gentle voice goes on.

"It is much better, I think, to go straight on with

what one is doing, without being continually deflected by outside people and happenings."

Our interested gaze persists. Suddenly an idea strikes me.

"But, suppose, Mac," I say, "that it was a *horse?*"

"Oh, a horse!" says Mac, becoming suddenly quite human and alive and not remote at all. "That would be *quite* different! Of course, I'd do everything I possibly could for a horse."

We all roar with laughter and he looks surprised.

Today has definitely been Constipation Day. Abd es Salaam's health has been for some days the burning topic. Every kind of aperient has been administered to him. As a result he is now, he says, "much weakened." "I should like to go into Kamichlie, Khwaja, and be pricked with a needle to restore my strength."

Even more parlous is the condition of one Saleh Hassan, whose inside has resisted all treatment, from a mild beginning with Eno's to a half-bottle of castor oil.

Max has recourse to the Kamichlie doctor's horse medicine. An enormous dose is administered, and Max then addresses the patient, telling him that if his inside "moves before sunset" a large bakshish will be given him.

His friends and relations forthwith rally round him. The afternoon is spent by them walking him round and round the mound, uttering encouraging cries and exhortations, whilst they keep an anxious eye fixed on the declining sun.

It is a near thing; but a quarter of an hour after Fidos we hear cheers and cries. The news goes round like wildfire! The floodgates have opened! Surrounded by an enthusiastic crowd, the pale sufferer is escorted to the house to receive his promised reward!

Subri, who is assuming more and more control, has taken the Brak establishment severely in hand, considering it is not nearly grand enough! He, like everyone else, is zealous for our "reputation." He persuades

Michel to forswear *economia* and buy soup-bowls in the Bazaar at Kamichlie. They and an enormous soup tureen make their appearance every evening, and take up far too much room on the one small table, so that everything else has to be balanced precariously on the bed! Ferhid's idea that you can help every dish and eat it with a knife has also been overruled, and a bewildering assortment of cutlery makes its appearance. Subri also gives Hiyou a bath, and combs out the knots in her hair with an immense comb (grudgingly bought by Michel), and even ties a bow of cheap pink satin round her neck. Hiyou is devoted to him!

The waterman's wife and three out of his ten children have arrived. ("Your doing," says Max to me reproachfully.) She is a whining and rather unpleasant woman, and the children are singularly unprepossessing. Their noses are, frankly, in a disgusting condition. Why should it be only the human young whose noses run when left in a state of nature? Young kittens, puppies, and donkeys do not seem to suffer from this affliction!

The grateful parents instruct their young to kiss the sleeves of their benefactors on every possible occasion, which they dutifully do, evading all efforts on our part to escape the ceremony! Their noses look much better afterwards, and I see Max looking down at his sleeve with a definite lack of confidence!

We hand out a fair amount of aspirin for headaches these days. It is very hot now and thundery. The men take advantage of both Eastern and Western science. Having swallowed our aspirins, they hurry off to the Sheikh, who obligingly places discs of red-hot metal on their foreheads "to drive out the evil spirit." I don't know who gets the credit of the cure!

A snake is discovered in our bedroom this morning by Mansur when he comes in to do his *"service."* It is coiled up in the basket under the washstand. Great excitement. All run and join in the kill. For the next three nights I listen apprehensively to rustlings before going to sleep. After that I forget.

I ask Mac at breakfast one morning if he would like a softer pillow, glancing at Bumps as I do so.

"I don't think so," says Mac, looking rather surprised. "Is anything wrong with mine?"

I throw Bumps a glance of triumph and he grins.

"I didn't believe you," he confesses afterwards. "I thought you were just making up a story about Mac, but he is incredible. Nothing he has or wears ever seems to get dirty or torn or untidy. And as you say, he's *nothing* in his room except his rug and his diary, not even a book. I don't know how he manages it."

I look round Bumps' half of the room he shares with the Colonel, which is strewn with the signs of his exuberant and overflowing personality. Only strenuous effort on the part of the Colonel avoids an overlap on to *his* side.

Michel suddenly begins hitting Mary with a large hammer just outside the window, and Bumps flies out like a rocket to tell him to stop!

Max and Bumps present a great contrast in costume now that the heat has come. Bumps has taken off everything that he can take off. Max, following Arab custom, has put on everything available. He is heavily dressed, with a very thick tweed coat pulled up round his neck, and does not seem to notice the sun at all.

Mac, we observe, is not even sunburnt!

The burning moment of "The Division" is now drawing very near. At the close of the season the Director of the Services des Antiquités comes up or sends a representative to divide all the season's finds.

In Iraq this used to be done object by object, and used to take several days.

In Syria, however, the system is much simpler. It is left to Max to arrange everything found in two parts exactly as he pleases. The Syrian representative then comes, examines the two collections, and selects which of them he will have for Syria. The other is then packed up for dispatch to the British Museum. Any particularly interesting objects, or anything unique, that may be in the Syrian half, is usually loaned by them, so that it can be studied, exhibited, photographed, etc., in London.

The real agony lies in making the two collections. You are bound to lose certain things you want desperately. Very well, then you must balance them on the other side. We all get called in to help Max as he deals with each class of object in turn. Two lots of celts, two lots of amulets, and so on. Pots, beads, bone objects, obsidian. Then, one by one, the rest of us are called in.

"Now, which lot of these two would you take? A or B."

Pause whilst I study the two.

"I'd take B."

"You would? All right. Send in Bumps."

"Bumps, A or B?"

"B."

"Colonel?"

"A, definitely."

"Mac?"

"I think B."

"Hm," says Max, "B's evidently too strong."

He removes a delightful little stone amulet of a horse's head from B to A, replaces it with a rather shapeless sheep, and makes a few more alterations.

We re-enter. This time we all plump for A.

Max tears his hair.

In the end we lose all sense of value and appearance.

Meanwhile all is feverish activity. Bumps and Mac are drawing like mad, and dashing to the mound to plan houses and buildings. The Colonel sits up into the night classifying and labelling those objects not yet done. I come and assist, and we disagree violently over nomenclature.

"Horse's head—steatite, 3 cms."

Me: "It's a *ram*."

"No, no, look at the *bridle*."

"That's the *horn*."

"Hi, Mac, what's this?"

Mac: "It's a gazelle."

Col.: "Bumps—what would you call this?"

Me: "A ram."

Bumps: "Looks like a *camel.*"

Max: "There weren't any camels. Camels are quite modern animals."

Col.: "Well, what do *you* say it is?"

Max: "Stylized bukranium!"

So it goes on, passing through various puzzling small amulets representing kidneys, and various obscure and ambiguous ones which are labelled discreetly by the convenient name of "cult object."

I am developing and printing and trying to keep the water cool. I do most of it early about six A.M. It is very hot now in the middle of the day.

Our workmen trickle away day after day.

"It is harvest now, Khwaja. We must go."

The flowers have long since disappeared, eaten by the pasturing cattle. All is now an even dim yellow on the mound. Round it, on the plain, are the corn and the barley. The crops this year are good.

At last the fateful day arrives. M. Dunand and his wife are arriving this evening. They are old friends of ours, whom we saw at Byblos when we were at Beyrout.

Evening comes; a superb (or what we think is superb) dinner is ready. Hiyou has been washed. Max is taking one last agonized look at the two shares spread out for display on long tables.

"I think that balances up. If we lose that lovely little horse's head amulet and that very uncommon cylinder seal (jolly interesting!), well, we shall get the best Chagar Mother Goddess and the double axe amulet, and that very fine incised pot. . . . But, of course, there's that early painted pot on the other side. Oh, hell, it will have to do now! Which would *you* choose!"

In common humanity we refuse to play further. We say we simply couldn't decide. Max murmurs sadly that Dunand is a very shrewd judge. "He'll have the better half all right."

We lead him away firmly.

The hours go on. Night falls. No sign of the Dunands.

"I wonder what can have happened to them," Max muses. "Of course, like everyone else out here, they drive at about ninety miles an hour. Hope there isn't an accident."

Ten o'clock, eleven o'clock. No Dunands.

Max queries whether they can possibly have gone to Brak instead of to Chagar.

"No, surely not. They know we're living here."

At midnight we give it up and go to bed. People do not motor much after dark in this part of the world.

Two hours later sounds of a car are heard. The boys run out and call us excitedly. We tumble out of bed, slip on something, and come out into the living-room.

It is the Dunands, and they have gone to Brak by an error. On leaving Hasetshe, they asked for a direction to "the digging of antiquities," and a man who had himself always worked at Brak directed them there. They lost their way, and were some time finding it. Once there, a guide came with them across country to show them the way to Chagar.

They have been motoring all day, but are quite cheerful and unruffled.

"You must have something to eat," says Max.

Madame Dunand says politely there is no need. A glass of wine and a biscuit—it will be quite sufficient.

At that moment Mansur enters, followed by Subri, and a whole four-course dinner makes its appearance! How the servants out here do that sort of thing I don't know. It seems a kind of miracle. We discover the Dunands have had nothing to eat and are really very hungry. We eat and drink far into the night, with Mansur and Subri standing beaming by.

As we are going to sleep Max says dreamily that he'd rather like to take Subri and Mansur to England. "They're so useful." I say I, too, would like to have Subri.

In the pause that follows I envisage the impact of Subri upon an English domestic household—his large knife, his oil-stained pullover and unshaven chin, his big echoing laugh. The fantastic uses to which he puts glasscloths!

Servants in the East are rather like *Jinns*. They appear from nowhere, and are there waiting for you when you arrive.

We never send word to tell of our coming, but sure enough, when we arrive, there is Dimitri. He has come all the way from the coast to be ready for us.

"How did you know we were coming?"

"It is known that there is to be digging again this year."

He adds gently: "It is very welcome. I have now the family of two of my brothers to support; there are eight children in one and ten in the other. They eat much. It is good to earn money. 'See,' I said to my brother's wife, 'God is good. We shall not starve this year—we are saved—the Khwajas are coming to dig!' "

Dimitri pads gently away, displaying his flower-patterned muslin trousers. His gentle meditative face beats the maternity of the Chagar Madonna to a frazzle. He loves puppies, kittens, and children. He alone of the servants never quarrels. He doesn't even *own* a knife except for culinary purposes.

All is over! The Division has taken place. M. and Madame Dunand have examined, handled, reflected. We have stood looking on in the usual agony. It takes M. Dunand about an hour to make up his mind. Then he flings a hand out in a quick Gallic gesture.

"*Eh bien,* I will take *this* one."

True to human nature, whichever half is chosen, we immediately wish it had been the other.

However, the suspense over, the atmosphere lifts. We are gay and the thing becomes a party. We go over the dig, examine the architects' plans and drawings, drive over to Brak, discuss work to be done the next season, and so on. Max and M. Dunand argue as to exact dates and sequences. Madame Dunand amuses us all by her dry witty remarks. We talk in French, though I fancy that she speaks English quite well. She is intensely amused by Mac and his stubborn limitation of conversation to *"Oui"* and *"Non."*

"Ah, votre petit architecte, il ne sait pas parler? Il a tout de même l'air intelligent!"

We repeat this to Mac, who is unperturbed.

On the next day the Dunands prepare for departure. Not that there is much preparation; they refuse food or drink to take with them.

"Surely you'll take *water!*" Max exclaims, brought up in the principle never to travel in these parts with no water.

They shake their heads carelessly.

"Suppose you had a breakdown?"

M. Dunand laughs and shakes his head.

"Oh, that will not happen!"

He lets in the clutch, and the car departs in the usual French desert style. Sixty miles an hour!

We no longer wonder at the high death rate for over-turned archaeologists in these parts!

And now, packing up once more—days of it! Crate after crate filled and fastened down and stencilled.

Then come the preparations for our own departure. We are going from Hasetshe by a little-used track through complete wilderness to the city of Raqqa on the Euphrates, and crossing the Euphrates there.

"And we shall be able," says Max, "to have a look at the Balikh!"

He says the word Balikh in the way he used to say Jaghjagha, and I perceive that he is forming plans to have just a little fun in the Balikh region before he finally leaves off digging in Syria.

"The Balikh?" I say innocently.

"Whacking great Tells all along it," says Max reverently.

X

THE TRAIL TO RAQQA

HERE WE GO! We are *off!*

The house is all boarded up, and Serkis is nailing the last planks across the windows and doors. The Sheikh stands by swelling with importance. All shall be secure until we return! The most trusted man of the village is to be our watchman! He shall guard it, says the Sheikh, night and day!

"Have no fear, brother!" he cries. "Even should I have to pay the man out of my own pocket, the house shall be guarded."

Max smiles, knowing quite well that the handsome remuneration already arranged with the watchman will probably go mostly into the Sheikh's pocket by way of rake-off.

"Everything will, indeed, be safe under your eye, we know," he replies. "The contents of the house will not easily deteriorate; and as for the outside, what pleasure it will be to us to hand it over to you in good condition when the day comes."

"May that day be long distant!" says the Sheikh.

"For when it comes, you will return no more, and that will be a sadness to me. You will perhaps dig only one more season?" he adds hopefully.

"One or two—who knows? It depends upon the work."

"It is regrettable that you have found no gold—only stones and pots," says the Sheikh.

"These things are of equal interest to us."

"Yet gold is always gold." The Sheikh's eyes glitter covetously. "In the days of El Baron——"

Max deftly interrupts:

"And when we return next season, what personal gift may I bring you from the city of London?"

"Nothing—nothing at all. I want nothing. A watch of gold is a pleasant thing to have."

"I shall remember."

"Let there be no talk of gifts between brothers! My only wish is to serve you and the Government. If I am out of pocket by so doing—well, to lose money in such a way is honorable."

"We should know no peace of heart unless we were quite sure that gain and not loss will be the result to you of our work here."

Michel comes up at this moment from where he has been nagging at everybody and shouting orders to say that all is in order and we can start.

Max checks up on the petrol and oil, and makes sure that Michel has with him the spare cans he has been told to have, and that no sudden qualms of *economia* have triumphed. Provisions, a supply of water, our luggage, the servants' luggage—yes, everything is there. Mary is loaded to bulging point both on the roof and inside, and perched amidst all are Mansur, Ali, and Dimitri. Subri and Ferhid return to Kamichlie, which is their home, and the foremen are going by train to Jerablus.

"Farewell, brother," cries the Sheikh, suddenly clasping the Colonel in his arms and embracing him on both cheeks.

Enormous joy of the whole Expedition!

The Colonel turns plum color.

The Sheikh repeats his salutation to Max and shakes the "Engineers" warmly by the hand.

Max, the Colonel, Mac, and myself get into Poilu. Bumps goes with Michel in Mary to curb any "good idea" Michel might have *en route*. Max reiterates his instructions to Michel. He is to follow us, but *not* at a distance of only three feet. If Michel tries to run down any parties of donkeys and old women on the road, half his salary will be stopped.

Michel murmurs "Mohammedans!" under his breath, but salutes and says in French: *"Très bien."*

"All right, off we go. Are we all here?"

Dimitri has two puppies with him. Hiyou is accompanying Subri.

"I will have her in splendid condition for you next year," Subri shouts.

"Where's Mansur?" shouts Max. "Where's that damned fool? We shall start without him if he doesn't come. Mansur!"

"Présent!" cries Mansur breathlessly, running into view. He is trailing two immense and horrible smelling sheepskins.

"You can't take those. Phew!"

"They will be worth money to me in Damascus!"

"What a reek!"

"The sun will dry them if they are spread on the top of Mary, and then they will not smell."

"They're disgusting. Leave 'em behind."

"He is right. They are worth money," says Michel. He climbs up on top of the lorry, and the skins are precariously lashed up with string.

"As the lorry is behind us we shan't smell them," says Max resignedly; "and anyway, they'll fall off before we get to Raqqa. Mansur tied one of those knots himself!"

"Ha, ha!" laughs Subri, throwing back his head, and showing his white and gold teeth. "Perhaps Mansur wants to make the trip on a horse!"

Mansur hangs his head. The staff have never stopped ragging him about his ride back from Kamichlie.

"Two gold watches," says the Sheikh in a meditative voice, "are a good thing to have. One can then lend one to a friend."

Max hurriedly gives the signal for departure.

We drive slowly through the cluster of houses and out on to the Kamichlie Hasetshe track. Crowds of small boys yell and wave.

As we drive through the next village of Hanzir, men run out from the houses and wave and shout. They are our old workmen.

"Come back next year," they yell.

"Inshallah!" Max yells back.

We drive along the track to Hasetshe, and look back for one last look at the mound of Chagar Bazar.

At Hasetshe we stop, buy bread and fruit, and go and wish the French officers good-bye. A young officer who has just come up from Der-ez-Zor interests himself in our journey.

"You go to Raqqa then? I will tell you. Do not follow the signpost when you come to it. Instead, take the track to the right of it and then the one that forks left. So you will have a straight track easy to follow. But the other way is most confusing."

The Capitaine, who has been listening, cuts in to say he strongly advises us to go north to Ras-el-Ain, then to Tell Abyadh, and take the well-frequented track from Tell Abyadh to Raqqa. Then there will be no mistake.

"But it is much longer, an immense way round."

"It may come shorter in the end."

We thank him, but persist in our original design.

Michel has made the necessary purchases and we start off, taking the bridge across the Habur.

We follow the young officer's advice when we come to a meeting-place of tracks with a signpost or two. One says Tell Abyadh, one Raqqa, and between them is one unmarked. That must be the one.

After a little distance along it the track divides into three.

"Left, I suppose," says Max, "or did he mean the middle one?"

We take the left-hand track, and after a little way it divides into four.

The country is now full of scrub and boulders. One has definitely to follow a track.

Max takes the left one again. "We should have taken the one to the extreme right," says Michel.

No one pays any attention to Michel, who has led us on more wrong tracks than we can possibly count.

I draw a veil over the next five hours. We are lost— lost in a part of the world where there are no villages, no cultivation, no Beduin pasturing—nothing.

The tracks deteriorate until they are hardly distinguishable. Max tries to take those leading roughly in the right direction—namely, a little west of south-west, but the tracks are perverse in the extreme. They twist and turn, and usually obstinately return due north.

We halt for a while and eat lunch and drink tea, which Michel makes. The heat is suffocating, the going is very bad. The jolting, the heat, and intense glare give me an excruciating headache. We all feel a little worried.

"Well," says Max, "we've got plenty of water at any rate. *What's that damned fool doing?*"

We turn. Mansur—the idiotic—is happily pouring out our precious water and sluicing it over his face and hands!

I pass over Max's language! Mansur looks surprised and a little aggrieved. He sighs. How difficult, he seems to be thinking, these people are to please. One's simplest action may annoy them.

We take the road again. The tracks turn and twist worse than ever. Sometimes they peter out altogether.

With a worried frown, Max mutters that we are going far too far north.

When the tracks divide now, they seem to run north and north-east. Shall we turn back altogether?

It is getting towards evening. Suddenly the quality of the ground improves, the scrub peters out, the stones are less plentiful.

"We've got to get somewhere," says Max. "I think we can go straight across country now."

"Where are you heading for?" asks the Colonel.

Max says due west for the Balikh. If we once strike the Balikh we shall find the main Tell Abyadh-Raqqa track and can go down it.

We drive on. Mary has a puncture and we lost precious time. The sun is setting.

Suddenly we see a welcome sight—men trudging ahead. Max lets out a whoop. He draws up beside them, giving greetings, asking questions.

The Balikh? The Balikh is just ahead of us. In ten minutes, in a machine like ours, we shall be there. Raqqa? We are nearer to Tell Abyadh than Raqqa.

Five minutes later we see a streak of green ahead— it is the vegetation bordering the river. A vast Tell looms up.

Max says ecstatically: "The Balikh—look at it! Tells everywhere!"

The Tells are indeed imposing—large, formidable, and very solid looking.

"Whacking great Tells," says Max.

I say disagreeably, because my head and eyes have reached an almost unbearable degree of pain: "Min Ziman er Rum."

"You're about right," says Max. "That *is* the snag. That solidity means Roman masonry—a chain of forts. The right stuff farther down, I've no doubt, but too long and expensive to get down to it."

I feel completely uninterested in archaeology. I want somewhere to lie down, and a great deal of aspirin and a cup of tea.

We come to a broad track running north and south, and turn South to Raqqa.

We are a long way out of our way, and it takes us an hour and a half before we see the city sprawling ahead of us. It is dark now. We drive into the outskirts.

It is an entirely native city—no European structures.
We ask for the Services Spéciaux. The officer there is
kind, but troubled for our comfort. There is no accommodation for travellers here. If we were to drive north
to Tell Abyadh? In two hours, if we drove fast, there
we should be really comfortable.

But nobody, least of all my suffering self, can bear
the thought of two more hours jolting and bouncing.
The kindly officer says there are two rooms—very
meagre, though, nothing European—but if we have our
own bedding? And our servants?

We arrive at the house in pitch-black darkness. Mansur and Ali run about with torches and light the primus
and spread out blankets and get in each other's way.
I long for the quick and efficient Subri. Mansur is incredibly slow and clumsy. Presently Michel comes in
and criticizes what Mansur is doing. Mansur stops and
they argue. I hurl all the Arabic I know at them. Mansur looks scared and resumes operations.

A roll of bedding and blankets is brought and I sink
down. Suddenly Max is beside me with the longed-for
cup of tea. He asks cheerfully if I feel bad. I say yes,
seize the tea, and swallow four aspirins. The tea tastes
like nectar. Never, never, *never* have I enjoyed anything so much! I sink back, my eyes close.

"Madame Jacquot," I murmur.

"Eh?" Max looks startled. He bends down. "What
did you say?"

"Madame Jacquot," I repeat.

The association is there—*I* know what I mean—but
the phrase has escaped me. Max has a kind of hospital
nurse's expression on his face—on no account con-
tradict the patient!

"Madame Jacquot's not here just now," he says in
a soothing tone.

I throw him an exasperated glance. My eyes are
gently closing. There is still a lot of bustle. A meal is
being prepared. Who cares? I am going to sleep—
sleep. . . .

Just as I am going off—the phrase comes. Of course!

"*Complètement knock out!*" I say with satisfaction.

"What?" says Max.

"Madame Jacquot," I say, and fall asleep.

The best of going to sleep utterly weary and pain-racked is the marvelous surprise you feel when you wake up well and energetic next morning.

I feel full of vigor and ferociously hungry.

"You know, Agatha," says Max, "I think you must have had fever last night. You were delirious. You kept talking about Madame Jacquot."

I throw him a scornful look and speak as soon as I can, my mouth being full of hard-fried egg.

"Nonsense!" I say at last. "If you'd only taken the trouble to *listen* you'd have known exactly what I meant! But I suppose your mind was so full of the Tells on the Balikh——"

"It would be interesting, you know," says Max, eager at once, "just to run a trial trench or two in some of those Tells. . . ."

Mansur comes up, beaming all over his stupid, honest face, and asks how the Khatūn is this morning.

I say I am very well. Mansur, it seems, is distressed because I was so fast asleep when supper was ready that nobody liked to wake me. Will I have another egg now?

"Yes," I say, having already eaten four. And this time, if Mansur fries it for about five minutes, it will be quite enough!

We start for the Euphrates about eleven. The river is very wide here, the country is pale and flat and shining, and the air is hazy. It is a kind of symphony in what Max would describe as "pinkish buff," if he were describing pottery.

To cross the Euphrates at Raqqa is a matter of a very primitive ferry. We join some other cars and settle down happily for an hour or two's wait until the ferry comes.

Some women come down to fill kerosene tins of water. Others are washing clothes. It is like a pattern on a frieze—the tall, black-clad figures, the lower half of the face covered, the heads very erect, the great dripping tins of water. The women move up and down, slow and unhurried.

I reflect enviously that it must be nice to have your face veiled. It must make you feel very private, very secret. . . . Only your eyes look out on the world—you see it, but it does not see you. . . .

I take out the glass from my hand-bag and open my powder compact. "Yes," I think, "it would be very nice to veil *your* face!"

Approaching civilization stirs within me. I begin to think of things. . . . A shampoo, a luxurious drier. Manicure . . . A porcelain bath with taps. Bath salts. Electric light . . . . More shoes!

"What's the matter with you?" says Max. "I've asked you twice whether you noticed that second Tell we passed on the road down from Tell Abyadh last night."

"I didn't."

"You didn't?"

"No. I wasn't noticing *anything* last night."

"It wasn't as solid a Tell as the others. Denudation on the east side of it. I wonder perhaps——"

I say clearly and firmly: "I'm tired of Tells!"

"What?" Max looks at me with the horror a medieval inquisitor might have felt on hearing a particularly flagrant bit of blasphemy.

He says: "You can't be!"

"I'm thinking of other things." I reel off a list of them, starting with electric light, and Max passes his hand over the back of his head and says he wouldn't mind having a decent haircut at last.

We all agree what a pity it is one can't go straight from Chagar to, say, the Savoy! As it is, the sharp pleasure of contrast is always lost. We go through a stage of indifferent meals and partial comfort so that the pleasure of switching on electric light or turning a tap is dulled.

Now the ferry is here. Mary is driven carefully up the inclined boards. Poilu follows.

We are out now on the broad Euphrates. Raqqa recedes. It looks beautiful, with its mud-brick and its Oriental shapes.

"Pinkish buff," I say softly.

"That striped pot, do you mean?"

"No," I say, "Raqqa. . . ."

And I repeat the name softly, like a good-bye, before I get back to the world where the electric light switch rules. . . .

Raqqa. . . .

XI

GOOD-BYE TO BRAK

NEW FACES AND old faces!

This is our last season in Syria. We are digging now at Tell Brak, having finally closed down at Chagar.

Our house, Mac's house, has been handed over (with immense ceremony) to the Sheikh. The Sheikh has already borrowed money on the house about three times over; nevertheless he displays distinct pride of ownership. To own the house will be good, we feel, for his "reputation."

"Though it will probably break his neck," says Max thoughtfully. He has explained to the Sheikh at length and with emphasis that the roof of the house must be seen to every year and duly repaired.

"Naturally, naturally!" says the Sheikh. "Inshallah, nothing will go wrong!"

"A bit too much Inshallah about it," says Max. "All Inshallah and no repairs! That's what will happen."

The house, a gaudy gold watch, and a horse have been presented to the Sheikh as gifts, exclusive of the rental due and compensation for crops.

Whether the Sheikh is a satisfied or a disappointed man we are not quite sure. He is all smiles and extravagant professions of affection, but he has a good try at getting extra compensation for "spoiling of the garden."

"What, then, is this garden?" asks the French officer, amused.

What indeed? Asked to produce any trace of ever having had a garden, and indeed of knowing what a garden *is,* the Sheikh climbs down. "I intended to produce a garden," he says austerely; "but by the digging my intention was foiled."

The "Sheikh's garden" is a subject of jest among us for some time.

This year we have at Brak with us the inevitable Michel; the gay Subri; Hiyou, with a litter of four hideous puppies; Dimitri, yearning tenderly over the puppies; and Ali. Mansur, the No. 1, the head boy, the servant skilled in European service, has, El hamdu lillah, joined the police force! He comes to see us one day, resplendent in uniform and grinning from ear to ear.

Guilford came out with us this spring as architect, and is with us again now. He has aroused enormous respect in me by being able to cut a horse's toe-nails.

Guilford has a long, fair, serious face, and was once, at the beginning of his first season, very particular about the careful sterilizing and application of dressings to the local cuts and wounds. Having seen, however, what happens to the dressings once the men get home, and having observed one Yusuf Abdullah remove a neat bandage and lie under the dirtiest corner of the dig letting sand trickle into his wound, Guilford now dabs on a good deal of permanganate solution (appreciated because of its rich hue!) and confines himself to emphasizing what is to be applied to the outside and what can safely be drunk.

The son of a local Sheikh, exercising a car after the manner of breaking-in a young horse, and having been overturned into a wadi, comes to Guilford for treatment

with an immense hole in his head. Horrified, Guilford
more or less fills it up with iodine, and the young man
staggers about, reeling with pain.

"Ah!" he gasps when he can speak. "That is fire
indeed! It is wonderful. In future I will always come
to you—never to a doctor. Yes—fire, fire, indeed!"

Guilford urges Max to tell him to go to a doctor,
as the wound is really serious.

"What—*this?*" demands the Sheikh's son scornfully.
"A headache, that is all! It is interesting, though," he
adds thoughtfully. "If I hold my nose and blow—so—
spittle comes out through the wound!"

Guilford turns green, and the Sheikh's son goes away
laughing.

He comes back four days later for further treatment.
The wound is healing with incredible rapidity. He is
deeply chagrined that no more iodine is applied; only
a cleansing solution.

"This does not burn at all," he says discontentedly.

A woman comes to Guilford with a pot-bellied child,
and whatever the real trouble, she is delighted at the
results of the mild medicaments given her. She returns
to bless Guilford "for saving the life of my son," and
adds that he shall have her eldest daughter as soon as
she is old enough; whereat Guilford blushes, and the
woman goes away, laughing heartily and making a few
final unprintable remarks. Needless to say she is a
Kurd, and not an Arab woman!

This is an autumn dig we are doing now to complete our work. This spring we finished Chagar and
concentrated on Brak, where many interesting things
were found. Now we are finishing up Brak, and are
going to end the season by a month or six weeks' digging at Tell Jidle, a mound on the Balikh!

A local Sheikh, whose camp is pitched near the Jaghjagha, invites us to a ceremonial feast, and we accept.
When the day comes, Subri appears in all the glory
of his tight plum suit, polished shoes, and Homburg
hat. He has been invited as our retainer, and he acts
s a go-between, reporting to us how the cooking of

the feast is proceeding and the exact moment at which our arrival should occur.

The Sheikh greets us with dignity under the wide, brown canopy of his open tent. There is a large following of friends, relations, and general hangers-on with him.

After courteous greetings, the great ones (ourselves, the foremen, Alawi and Yahya, the Sheikh and his chief friends) all sit down in a circle. An old man, handsomely apparelled, approaches us, bearing a coffee-pot and three little cups. A tiny drop of intensely black coffee is poured into each. The first one is handed to *me*—proof that the Sheikh is acquainted with the (extraordinary!) European custom of serving women first. Max and the Sheikh have the next two. We sit and sip. In due course another tiny drop is poured into our cups and we continue to sip. Then the cups are taken back, refilled, and Guilford and the foreman drink in their turn. So it goes on round the circle. A little distance away stands a considerable crowd of those of the second rank. From behind the partition of the tent close beside me come muffled giggles and rustlings. The Sheikh's womenfolk are peeping and listening to what goes on.

The Sheikh gives an order, and a follower goes out and returns with a perch, on which is a handsome falcon. This is set in the middle of the tent. Max congratulates the Sheikh upon the magnificent bird.

Then three men appear, carrying a large copper cauldron, which is set down in the middle of the circle. It is full of rice, on which is laid pieces of lamb. All is spiced and smoking hot and smelling delicious. Courteously we are invited to eat. We have flaps of Arab bread, with which and our fingers we help ourselves from the dish.

In due course (which is not for some time, let me say) hunger and politeness are satisfied. The vast platter, with its choicest morsels gone but still more than half-full, is lifted up and set down a little farther along, where a second circle (including Subri) sit down to eat.

Sweetmeats are handed to us and more coffee is served.

After the secondary folk have satisfied their hunger, the platter is set down in yet a third place. Its contents now are mainly rice and bones. The complete inferiors sit down to this, and those who, destitute, have come to "sit in the shadow of the Sheikh." They fling themselves upon the food, and when the platter is lifted it is quite empty.

We sit a little longer, Max and the Sheikh exchanging grave comments at intervals. Then we rise, thank the Sheikh for his hospitality, and depart. The coffee-server is handsomely remunerated by Max, and the foremen single out certain mysterious individuals as those to whom *largesse* is due.

It is hot, and we walk home, feeling quite dazed with rice and mutton. Subri is highly satisfied with the entertainment. All, he considers, has been conducted with strict propriety.

Today, a week later, we in our turn have entertained a visitor. This is none other than a Sheikh of the Shammar tribe—a very great man indeed. Local Sheikhs were in attendance on him and he arrived in a beautiful grey car. A very handsome and sophisticated person, with a dark thin face and beautiful hands.

Our European meal was the best we could make it, and the excitement of the staff at the consequence of our visitor was immense!

When he finally drove away, we felt as though we had been entertaining the royal family at least.

Today has been a day of catastrophe.

Max goes in to Kamichlie with Subri for shopping and to transact business with the Bank, leaving Guilford planning buildings on the mound and the foremen in charge of the men.

Guilford comes home to lunch, and he and I have just finished, and he is about to take Poilu back again

to the work when we notice that the foremen are running towards the house as fast as they can come with
every sign of agitation and distress.

They burst into the courtyard and pour out a flood
of excited Arabic.

Guilford is completely blank, and I understand about
one word in seven.

"Somebody's dead," I say to Guilford.

Alawi repeats his story with emphasis. Four people,
I gather, are dead. I think at first that this has been
a quarrel and the men have killed each other, but
Yahya shakes his head emphatically at my halting questions.

I curse myself for not having learnt to understand
the language! My Arabic consists almost entirely of
phrases like "This is not clean. Do it like this. Do not
use that cloth. Bring in tea," and such domestic orders.
This recital of violent death is quite beyond me. Dimitri
and the boy and Serkis come out and listen. They understand what has happened, but since they can speak
no European language, Guilford and I are still no
wiser.

Guilford says: "I'd better go up and see," and moves
towards Poilu.

Alawi grabs him by the sleeve and speaks vehement-
ly, evidently dissuading him. He points dramatically.
Down the sides of Brak, a mile away, a mob of motley
and white-robed figures are pouring, and there is somehow an ugly and purposeful look about them. The foremen, I see, are looking frightened.

"These fellows have run away," says Guilford
sternly. "I wish we could understand what the trouble
is."

Has Alawi (hot tempered) or Yahya killed a workman with a pick? It seems wildly unlikely, and certainly
they could not have killed *four*.

I suggest again haltingly that there has been a fight,
and illustrate in dumb show. But the response is emphatically negative. Yahya gestures to something coming down from above his head.

I look up at the sky. Have the victims been struck down by a thunderbolt?

Guilford opens the door of Poilu. "I'm going up to see, and these fellows must come with me."

He beckons them in authoritatively. Their refusal is prompt and decisive. They are not coming.

Guilford sticks an aggressive Australian chin out. "They've *got* to come!"

Dimitri is shaking his large gentle head.

"No, no," he says. "It is very bad."

"*What* is very bad?"

"There's some kind of trouble up there," says Guilford. He jumps into the car. Then, as he looks at the rapidly approaching mob, his head turns sharply. He stares at me in consternation, and I see what may be described as the "women-and-children-first" look come into his eyes.

He descends from the car, taking care to make the movement leisurely, and says in a careful holiday tone:

"How about taking a spin along the road to meet Max? Might as well, as there is no work going on. You get your hat or whatever you want."

Dear Guilford, he is doing it beautifully! So careful not to alarm me.

I say slowly that we might as well, and shall I bring the money? The expedition money is kept in a cash-box under Max's bed. If we really have an infuriated mob coming to attack the house, it will be a pity if they find money to steal.

Guilford, still trying not to "alarm me," pretends that this is quite an everyday suggestion.

"Could you," he says, "be rather *quick?*"

I go into the bedroom, pick up my felt hat, drag out the cash-box, and we lift it into the car. Guilford and I get in, and we beckon to Dimitri and Serkis and the boy to get in at the back.

"We'll take them and not the foremen," says Guilford, still condemnatory of the latter's attitude in "running away."

I am sorry for Guilford, who is obviously longing

to go and face the mob, and has instead to care for my safety. But I am very glad that he is not going to the men. He has very little authority with them, and will, in any case, not understand a word they say, and he may easily make matters very much worse. What we need is to get Max on to the matter and find out what has really *happened*.

Guilford's plan for saving Dimitri and Serkis and leaving the foremen to deal with their responsibilities is at once circumvented by Alawi and Yahya, who push aside Dimitri and climb into the car. Guilford is furious and tries to eject them. They refuse to budge.

Dimitri nods his head placidly and gestures to the kitchen. He walks back and Serkis goes with him, looking a little unhappy about it.

"I don't see why these fellows——" begins Guilford.

I interrupt.

"We can only take four in the car—and actually it seems to be Alawi and Yahya whom the men want to kill if anybody, so I think we'd better take them. I don't think the men will have anything against Dimitri and Serkis."

Guilford looks up and sees that the running mob is getting too near for more argument. He scowls at Yahya and Alawi and drives rapidly out through the courtyard gate and round by the village to the track which leads to the Kamichlie road.

Max must have started back by now since he intended to be on the work early this afternoon, so we ought to meet him before long.

Guilford draws a sigh of relief and I tell him that that was very nicely done.

"What was?"

"Your casual suggestion of a pleasant drive to meet Max, and the way you avoided alarming me."

"Oh," says Guilford; "so you realized I wanted to get you away?"

I look at him pityingly.

We drive at full speed and in about a quarter of an hour we meet Max returning with Subri in Mary. Very surprised to see us, he pulls up. Alawi and Yahya pour themselves out of Poilu and rush towards him, and an excited spate of Arabic fills the air as Max asks sharp staccato questions.

Now at last we learn what it is all about!

For some days past we have been finding a large number of very beautifully carved small animal amulets in stone and ivory in a certain part of the dig. The men have been getting high bakshish for these, and in order to find as many as they can they have been undercutting in the pit where they are, since the amulets are at a level some way down.

Yesterday Max stopped this, since it was getting dangerous, and put the gangs to work on top again to cut down from there. The men grumbled, since it meant that they would have a day or two's digging of uninteresting levels before they came to the amulet level once more.

The foremen were put on guard to see that they obeyed orders, and actually, although they were sulky about it, they did what they were told, and started working from the top as vigorously as possible.

This was the position when work was knocked off for lunch. And now comes a tale of base treachery and greed. The men were all stretched out on the hillside near the water jars. A gang of men who had been working on the other side crept away, sneaked round the mound to the rich spot, and began furiously digging in at the already undercut spot. They were going to rob the other men's pitch, and pretend to produce the filched objects from their own patch of ground.

And then Nemesis overcame them. They undercut too far, and down came the higher levels on top of them!

The yells of the one man who escaped brought the whole crowd running to the spot. At once they and the foremen realized what had occurred, and three pickmen began hurriedly to dig their comrades out. One man was alive, but four others were dead.

Wild excitement rose at once. Cries, lamentations to

Heaven, and a desire to blame someone. Whether the foremen lost their nerve and decided to run away, or whether they were actually attacked, is hard to make out. But the result was, that the men poured after them in a suddenly nasty mood.

Max inclines to the view that the foremen lost their nerve and put the idea of attacking them into the men's heads, but he wastes no time in recrimination. He turns the cars, and we both drive for all we are worth towards Kamichlie, where Max lays the matter at once before the officer at the Services Spéciaux who is in charge of security.

The Lieutenant is quick to comprehend and act. He collects four soldiers and his car and we all drive back to Brak. The men are on the mound now, seething and swaying rather like a swarm of bees. They subside when they see authority approaching. We walk up the mound in a procession. The Lieutenant sends his car off with one of the soldiers, and he himself goes to the scene of the tragedy.

Here he inquires into the facts, and the men whose place it properly is explain that it was not they but a rival gang who were trying to steal a march on them. The survivor is then interrogated, and confirms this story. Are these all the men of the gang? One unhurt, one injured and four dead? There is no possibility of any one still being buried? No.

At this point the Lieutenant's car returns with the local Sheikh of the tribe to which the dead workmen belong. He and the Lieutenant take charge together. Question and answer goes on.

Finally the Sheikh raises his voice and addresses the crowd. He absolves the Expedition of all blame. The men were digging out of work hours in their own time, and were, moreover, endeavoring to steal from their comrades. Theirs has been the reward of disobedience and greed. Everyone is now to go home.

The sun has set by this time and night is falling.

The Sheikh, the Lieutenant, and Max drive down to

the house (where we are relieved to find Dimitri placidly cooking dinner and Serkis grinning).

Consultations proceed for about an hour. The incident is regrettable. The Lieutenant says that the men have families, and although there is no obligation, doubtless a donation would be appreciated. The Sheikh says that generosity is the hallmark of a noble nature, and will much enhance our reputation in the countryside.

Max says that he would like to make a gift to the families, if it is clearly understood that it *is* a gift, and not in any sense compensation. The Sheikh grunts earnest agreement. That shall be set down in writing by the French officer, he says. Moreover, he will himself make it known on his word. The question remains of how much. When that has been adjusted and refreshments have been served, the Sheikh and the Lieutenant depart. Two soldiers are left on the mound to guard the fatal spot.

"And mind," says Max as we go very tired to bed, "someone's got to watch that spot to-morrow at lunchtime or we'll have the same thing happening again."

Guilford is incredulous.

"Not after they know the danger and have seen what happened!"

Max says grimly: "Wait and see!"

On the next day he himself waits inconspicuously behind a mud-brick wall. Sure enough, whilst lunch is in progress, three men come stealing round the slope of the mound and start furious scrabbling at the adjoining portion of the excavation not two feet from where their comrades were killed!

Max strides forth and delivers a terrific harangue. Do they not realize that what they are doing will bring death?

One of the men murmurs "Inshallah!"

They are then formally sacked for attempting to steal from their companions.

After that the spot is guarded after Fidos until the

moment when, on the following afternoon, the top levels
have been cut down.

Guilford says in a horrified voice:

"These fellows don't seem to have any care for their
lives at all. And they are extraordinarily callous. They
were laughing about the deaths and making dumb show
of the whole thing this morning during the work!"

Max says death isn't really important out here.

The foremen's whistle blows for Fidos, and the men
run down the mound past us singing: *"Yusuf Daoud
was with us yesterday—today he is dead! He will not
fill his belly any more. Ha, ha, ha!"*

Guilford is profoundly shocked.

XII

AIN EL ARUS

HOUSE-MOVING FROM Brak to the Balikh.

We walk down to the Jaghjagha on our last evening and feel a gentle melancholy. I have come to have a great affection for the Jaghjagha, that narrow stream of muddy brown water.

Still, Brak has never had the hold on my affections that Chagar has. The village of Brak is melancholy, half deserted and tumbling down, and the Armenians in their seedy European clothes look out of tune with the surroundings. Their voices rise scoldingly, and there is none of the rich Kurdish and Arabic joy of life. I miss the Kurdish women strolling across the countryside—those great gay flowers, with their white teeth and their laughing faces, and their proud, hand-some carriage.

We have hired a ramshackle lorry to take what fur-niture we shall need. It is the kind of lorry where everything has to be tied on with string! I have an idea that nearly everything will have dropped off by the time we get to Ras-el-Ain.

All is loaded up at last and we start off, Max Guilford and I in Mary, and Michel and the servants in Poilu with Hiyou.

Halfway to Ras-el-Ain we halt for a picnic lunch, and find Subri and Dimitri in roars of laughter. "Hiyou," they say, "has been sick all the way, and Subri has been holding her head!" The inside of Poilu bears eloquent testimony to this story! It is fortunate, I reflect, that it strikes them as funny.

Hiyou, for the first time I have known her, looks defeated. "I can face," she seems to say, "a hostile world to dogs, the enmity of the Moslem people, death by drowning, semi-starvation, blows, kicks, stones. I fear nothing. I am friendly to all but love nobody. But what is this strange new affliction that takes from me all my self-respect?" Her amber eyes go mournfully from one to the other of us. Her faith in her ability to meet the worst the world can do is shattered.

Happily, five minutes later, Hiyou is restored to her normal self, and is devouring immense quantities of Subri's and Dimitri's lunch. I ask if this is really wise, pointing out that the car journey will soon be resumed.

"Ha," cries Subri, "then Hiyou will be sick a great deal more!"

Well, if it amuses them. . . .

We arrive at our house early in the afternoon. It is in one of the main streets of Tell Abyadh. It is an almost urban dwelling; what the Bank Manager calls a "construction en pierre." There are trees all down the street, and their leaves are brilliant now in autumn coloring. The house, alas, is very damp, being below street level, and the village has streams everywhere. In the morning one's top blanket is quite wet, and everything you touch feels damp and clammy. I get so stiff I can hardly move.

There is a pleasant little garden behind the house, and it is much more sophisticated than anywhere we have lived for a long time.

We have lost three chairs, a table, and my lavatory seat from the lorry when it arrives! A good deal less than I thought we should!

Tell Jidle itself is set by a big pool of azure-blue water formed by the spring which feeds the Balikh. It has trees round the pool and is really a lovely spot and is the traditional meeting-place of Isaac and Rebecca. This is all very different from where we have been before. It has a lovely but melancholy charm, but none of the untouched freshness of Chagar and the rolling country round it.

There is a lot of prosperity here, well-dressed Armenians and others walk along the streets, and there are houses and gardens.

We have been there a week when Hiyou disgraces us. All the dogs of Ain el Arus arrive to woo her, and since none of the doors shut properly it is impossible to keep them out or her shut up! There is howling, barking, and fighting. Hiyou, a pensive amber-eyed belle, does everything to encourage the pandemonium!

The scene is exactly like that of an old-fashioned pantomime when demons pop out from windows and trap-doors. As we sit at supper a window flies open and a large dog leaps in, another leaps after it in pursuit—crash! The bedroom door flies open and another dog appears. All three rush madly round the table, charge Guilford's door, burst it open, and disappear, to reappear like magic through the door from the kitchen with a frying-pan hurled after them by Subri.

Guilford spends a sleepless night, with dogs bursting in at the door, over his bed, and out through the window. At intervals Guilford gets up and flings things after them. There are howls, yelps, and general dog saturnalia!

Hiyou, herself, we discover, is a snob. She favors the only dog in Ain el Arus who wears a collar! "Here," she seems to say, "is real *class!*" He is a black dog, snub-nosed, and with an immense tail rather like a funeral horse.

Subri, after spending sleepless nights with tooth-ache, demands leave of absence to go to Aleppo by train and visit the dentist. He returns two days later beaming.

His account of the proceedings is as follows:

"I go to the dentist. I sit in his chair. I show him the tooth. Yes, he says, it must come out. How much, I say? Twenty francs, he says. It is absurd, I say, and I leave the house. I come again in the afternoon. How much? Eighteen francs. Again I say absurd. All the time the pain is increasing, but one cannot allow one-self to be robbed. I come the next morning. How much? Still eighteen francs. Again at midday? Eighteen francs. He thinks that the pain will beat me, but I continue to bargain! In the end, Khwaja, I *win*."

"He comes down?"

Subri shakes his head.

"No, he will not come down, but I make a very good bargain. Very well, I say. Eighteen francs. But for that you must take out not one tooth but four!"

Subri laughs with enormous gusto, displaying sundry gaps.

"But did the other teeth ache?"

"No, of course not. But they will begin to some day. Now they cannot. They have been taken out, and for the price of one."

Michel, who has been standing in the doorway listen-ing, now nods his head approvingly. "Beaucoup econo-mia," he says.

Subri has kindly brought back a string of red beads, which he ties round Hiyou's neck. "It is what the girls put on to show they are married," he says. "And Hiyou, she has lately been married."

She certainly has! To every dog in Ain el Arus, I should say!

This morning, which is a Sunday and our day off, I am sitting labelling finds, and Max is writing up the

pay-book, when a woman is shown in by Ali. She is
a most respectable-looking woman, dressed neatly in
black, with an enormous gold cross on her bosom. Her
lips are tightly pressed together and she looks very
upset.

Max greets her politely, and she begins at once to
pour out a long tale, evidently of woe. Now and then
Subri's name enters the narrative. Max frowns and
looks grave. The tale goes on, getting even more impassioned.

I surmise that this is the old and well-known tale of
betrayal of the village maiden. This woman is the
mother, and our gay Subri is the base deceiver.

The woman's voice rises in righteous indignation.
She clasps the cross on her breast with one hand and
holds it up, and appears to be swearing something on
it.

Max calls for Subri to be sent in. I think that perhaps it would be more delicate if I withdrew, and I
am just about to edge out unobtrusively when Max
tells me to stay where I am. I sit down again, and since
I am presumably required to give the effect of a witness, look as though I understand what it is all about.

The woman, a grave, dignified figure, stands silent
until Subri appears. Then she flings out a hand of de-
nunciation, and evidently repeats her accusation against
him.

Subri does not defend himself with any vigor. He
shrugs his shoulders, raises his hands, appears to admit
the truth of the indictment.

The drama goes on—argument, recrimination, the
adoption of a more and more judicial attitude by Max.
Subri is being defeated. Very well, he seems to be saying, do as you like!

Suddenly Max pulls a sheet of paper towards him
and writes. He puts the written words in front of the
woman. She puts a mark—a cross—on the paper, and,
holding up the gold cross once more, swears some
solemn oath. Max then signs, and Subri also makes his
mark, and swears apparently some oath of his own.

Max then counts out some money and gives it to the woman. She takes it, thanks Max with a dignified inclination of the head, and goes out. Max addresses some biting reproaches to Subri, who goes out looking very much deflated.

Max leans back in his chair, passes a handkerchief over his face, and says "Whoof!"

I burst into speech.

"What was it all about? A girl? Was it the woman's daughter?"

"Not exactly. That was the local brothel-keeper."

"What?"

Max gives me as nearly as possible the woman's own words.

She has come to him, she says, so that he can redress a grievous wrong done to her by his servant Subri.

"What has Subri done?" Max asks.

"I am a woman of character and honor. I am respected throughout the district! All speak well of me. My house is conducted in a God-fearing manner. Now comes this fellow, this Subri, and he finds in my house a girl whom he has known in Kamichlie. Does he renew his acquaintance with her in a pleasant and decorous manner? No, he acts lawlessly, violently—in a way to bring disrepute on me! He flings down the stairs and out of the house a Turkish gentleman—a rich Turkish gentleman, one of my best patrons. All this he does violently and in an unseemly fashion! Moreover, he persuades the girl, who owes me money and has received much kindness from me, to leave my house. He buys a ticket for her and sends her away on the train. Moreover, she takes with her one hundred and ten francs that belong to me, which is robbery! Now, Khwaja, it is not right that such abuses should be done. I have been an upright and virtuous woman always, a God-fearing widow, against whom none can speak. I have struggled long and hard against poverty, and have raised myself in the world by my own honest efforts. It cannot be that you will take the side of violence and wrong. I ask for retribution, and I swear to you (this was the point where the gold cross came into play) that all I have said is true, and I will repeat it to your servant Subri's face. You can ask of the Magistrate, of the Priest, of the French officers of the garrison—all will tell you that I am an honest and a respectable woman!"

Subri, summoned, denies nothing. Yes, he had known the girl in Kamichlie. She was a friend of his. He had got annoyed with the Turk and pushed him downstairs. And he had suggested to the girl that she should go back to Kamichlie. She preferred Kamichlie to Ain el Arus. The girl had borrowed a little money to take with her, but doubtless all would be repaid some day.

It was then left to Max to pronounce judgment.

"Really, the things one has to do in this country. You never know what is coming next," he groans.

I ask him what his judgment has been.

Max clears his throat and goes on with his recital.

"I am surprised and displeased that a servant of mine should have entered your house, for that does not accord with our honor, the honor of the Expedition, and it is my command that none of my servants shall enter your house in future, so let this be clearly understood!"

Subri says gloomily it is understood.

"As to the matter of the girl leaving your house, I will take no action, for it is not any concern of mine. For the money that she took with her—that, I consider, should be repaid to you, and I will repay it to you now, for the honor of the servants of the Expedition. The sum shall be stopped out of Subri's wages. I will write a paper, which I will read you, acknowledging the payment of this money and repudiating any other claim upon us. You shall make your mark upon it, and you shall swear that this is the end of the matter."

I recall the dignity and Biblical fervor with which the woman had held up the cross.

"Did she say anything more?"

"I thank you, Khwaja. Justice and truth have prevailed as they always do, and evil has not been allowed to triumph."

"Well," I say, rather overcome. *"Well . . ."*

I hear light footsteps tripping past the window.

It is our late guest. She carries a large missal or prayerbook and is just going to church. Her face is grave and decorous. The large cross bobs up and down on her breast.

Presently I get up, take the Bible from the shelf, and turn to the story of Rahab the harlot. I feel I know—a little—what Rahab the harlot was like. I can see this woman playing that part—zealous, fanatical, courageous; deeply religious, and nevertheless—Rahab the harlot.

December is upon us; the end of the season has come. Perhaps because it is autumn and we are used to spring, perhaps because already rumors and warnings of European unrest are in the air, there has been a touch of sadness. There is the feeling, this time, that we may not come back. . . .

Yet the Brak house is still rented—our furniture will be stored there, and there is still plenty to be found in the mound. Our lease runs for two years. Surely we shall come back. . . .

Mary and Poilu take the road through Jerablus to Alep. From Alep we go to Ras Shamra, and spend Christmas with our friends, Professor and Madame Schaeffer, and their very delightful children. There is no spot in the world more charming than Ras Shamra, a lovely little bay of deep-blue water framed in white sand and low white rocks. They give us a wonderful Christmas. We talk of next year—some year. But the feeling of uncertainty grows. We say good-bye to them. "We shall meet again in Paris."

Alas, Paris!

We leave Beyrout by boat this time.

I stand looking over the rail. How lovely it is, this coast with the mountains of the Lebanon standing up dim and blue against the sky! There is nothing to mar the romance of the scene. One feels poetical, almost sentimental. . . .

A familiar hubbub breaks out—excited cries from a cargo boat we are passing. The crane has dropped a load into the sea, the crate has burst open. . . .

The surface of the sea is dotted with lavatory seats. . . .

Max comes up and asks what the row is about? I point, and explain that my mood of romantic farewell to Syria is now quite shattered!

Max says he had no idea we exported them in such quantities! And he shouldn't have thought there was enough plumbing in the country to connect them up to!

I fall silent, and he asks me what I am thinking of?

I am remembering how the carpenter at Amuda set up my lavatory seat proudly by the front door when the nuns and the French Lieutenant came to tea. I am remembering my towel-horse with its "beautiful feet"! And the professional cat! And Mac walking up and down the roof at sunset with a happy remote face. . . .

I am remembering the Kurdish women at Chagar like gay striped tulips. And the vast henna red beard of the Sheikh. I am remembering the Colonel, kneeling with his little black bag to attend at the uncovering of a burial, and a wag among the workmen saying: "Here is the doctor come to attend the case," so that ever afterwards "M. le docteur" becomes the Colonel's nickname. I am remembering Bumps and his recalcitrant topee, and Michel crying *"Forca"* as he pulls on the straps. I am remembering a little hill all covered with golden marigolds where we had a picnic lunch on one of our holidays; and closing my eyes, I can smell, all round me, the lovely scent of flowers and of the fertile steppe. . . .

"I am thinking," I say to Max, "that it was a very happy way to live. . . ."

EPILOGUE

THIS INCONSEQUENT CHRONICLE was begun before the war, and was started for the reasons I have stated.

Then it was laid aside. But now, after four years of war, I have found my thoughts turning more and more to those days spent in Syria, and at last I have felt impelled to get out my notes and rough diaries and complete what I had begun and laid aside. For it seems to me that it is good to remember that there were such days and such places, and that at this very minute my little hill of marigolds is in bloom, and old men with white beards trudging behind their donkeys may not even know there is a war. *"It does not touch us here. . . ."*

For after four years spent in London in war-time, I know what a very good life that was, and it has been a joy and refreshment to me to live those days again. . . . Writing this simple record has been not a task, but a labor of love. Not an escape to something that was, but the bringing into the hard work and sorrow of today of something imperishable that one not only *had* but still *has!*

For I love that gentle fertile country and its simple people, who know how to laugh and how to enjoy life; who are idle and gay, and who have dignity, good manners, and a great sense of humor, and to whom death is not terrible.

Inshallah, I shall go there again, and the things that I love shall not have perished from this earth. . . .

Spring, 1944.

FINIS

EL HAMDU LILLAH

Mystery, Christie Style

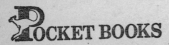

POCKET BOOKS

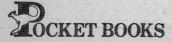